Emily Carr

On the Edge of Nowhere

Mary Jo Hughes • Kerry Mason

THE ART GALLERY OF GREATER VICTORIA

Library and Archives Canada Cataloguing in Publication

Hughes, Mary Jo
Emily Carr : on the edge of nowhere /
Mary Jo Hughes and Kerry Mason.

Includes bibliographical references.
Catalogue of an exhibition held at the
Art Gallery of Greater Victoria,
Victoria. B.C., from June 30, 2010-
ISBN 978-0-88885-360-8

1. Carr, Emily, 1871-1945—Exhibitions. 2. Art Gallery of Greater Victoria—Exhibitions. I. Carr, Emily, 1871-1945 II. Mason, Kerry Louise, 1950- III. Art Gallery of Greater Victoria IV. Title.

ND249.C3A4 2010 759.11 C2010-902205-X

Printed in Canada

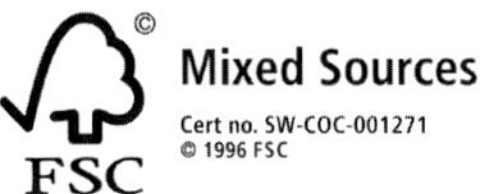

COVER:
Sea and Sky, (detail front), 1933, oil on paper
59.5 x 88.0 cm, The Art Gallery of Greater Victoria,
Anonymous Gift 1977.162.001

OPPOSITE:
Emily Carr in Her Studio, 1936,
Photo by Harold Mortimer Lamb
The Art Gallery of Greater Victoria,
Harold & Vera Mortimer Lamb Purchase Fund
1980.087.03

NEXT SPREAD:
Odds and Ends, 1939, oil on canvas, 67.4 x 109.5 cm,
Formerly in the collection of the Greater Victoria Public Library.
Transferred to the Art Gallery of Greater Victoria. This has been
made possible through a fund, given by an anonymous donor to the
Victoria foundation for the benefit of the Greater Victoria Public Library
1998.001.001

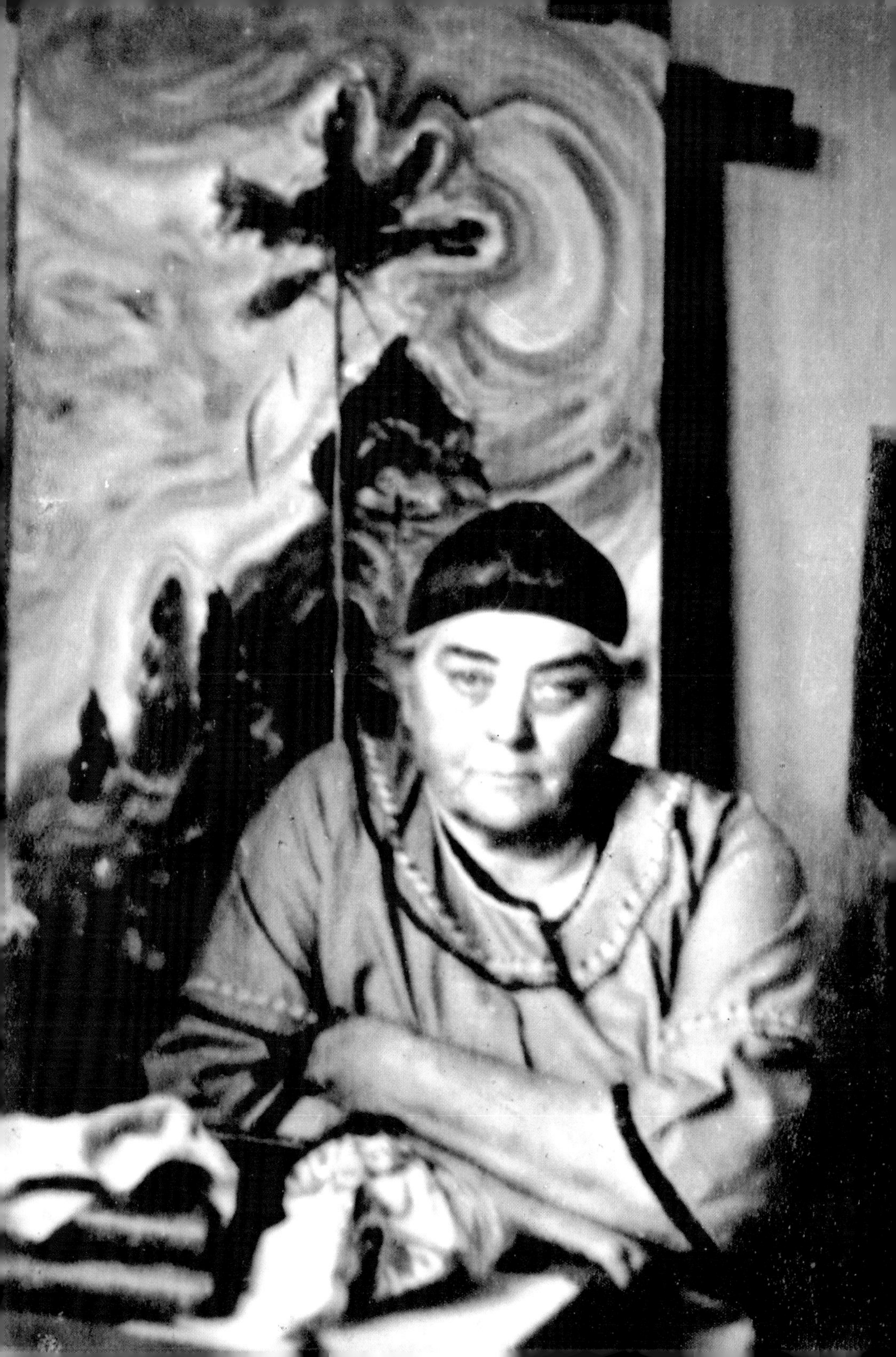

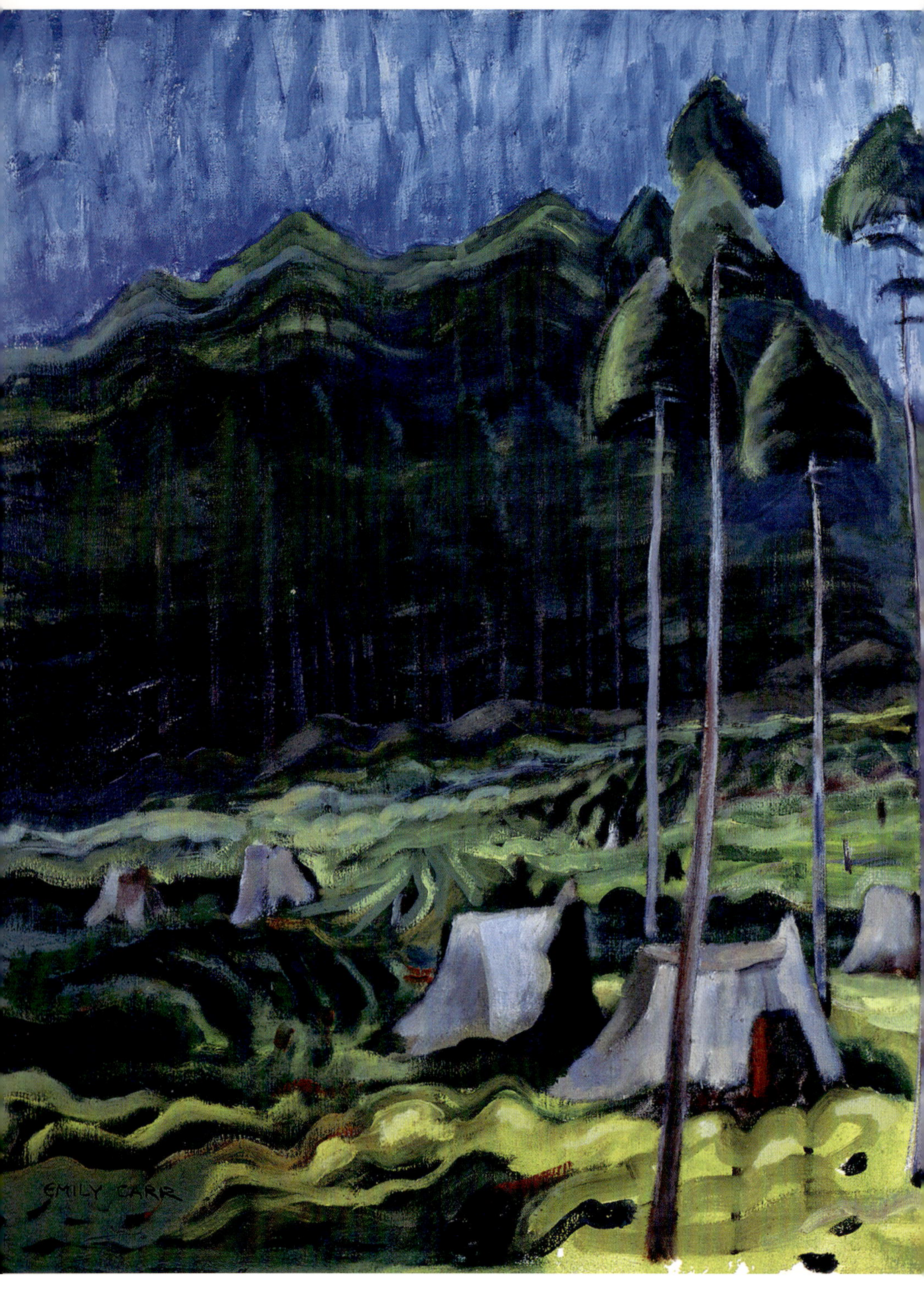
EMILY CARR

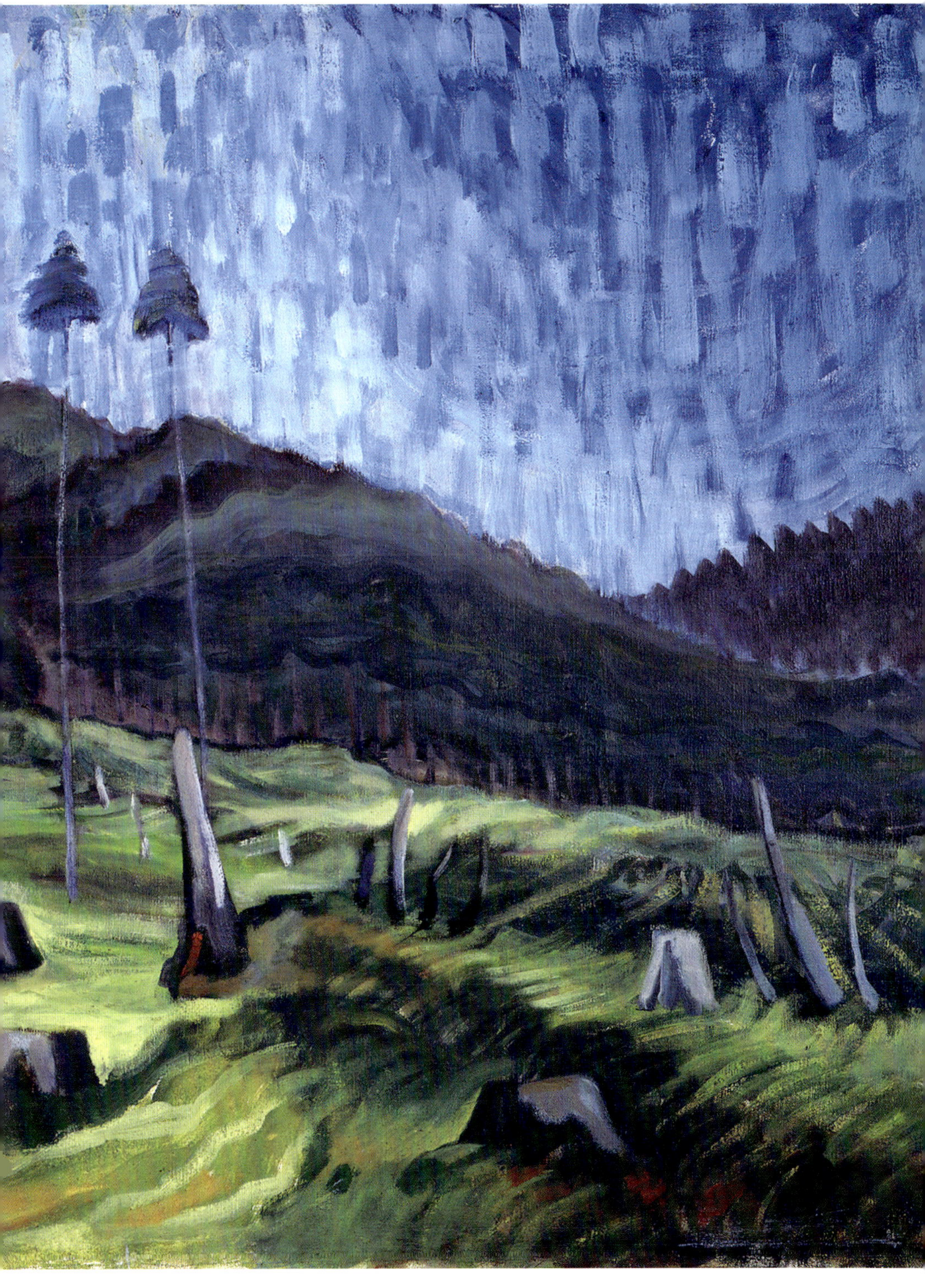

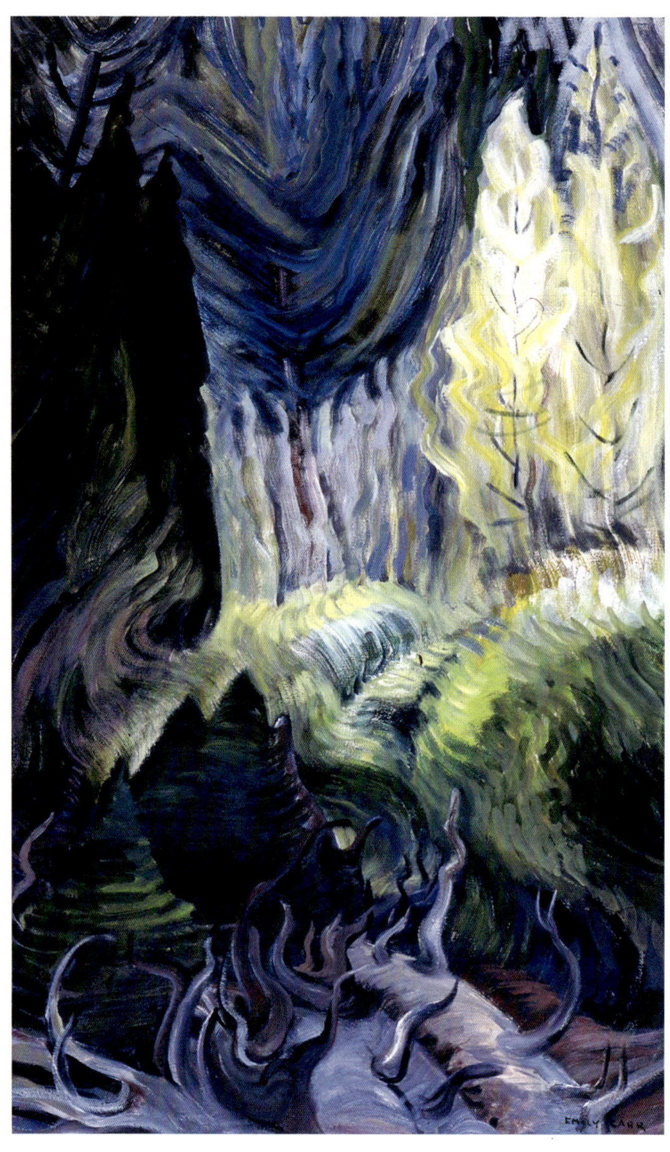

Light Swooping Through, 1938-1939, oil on canvas, 111.0 x 68.5 cm
The Art Gallery of Greater Victoria, Gift of the Hon. Mark Kearley 1964.229.001

Director's Foreword

When Emily Carr died in 1945, her hometown of Victoria did not have a public art gallery. As a result, most of the artworks that were in her estate went to the Vancouver Art Gallery to be held in trust for the benefit of the citizens of British Columbia. Six years later, when the permanent site of the Art Gallery of Greater Victoria was established on Moss Street, there was not one work by Victoria's most renowned artist in the permanent collection. It would not be until 1964 that any of Carr's work was acquired. These first donations were from two founders of the Gallery: Major H.C. Holmes and Mark Kearley. Over the succeeding decades, the Art Gallery has gradually accumulated a remarkable selection of Carr's works that now allows us to present an exhibition that touches upon all the significant periods of her career. The growth of this collection is due almost entirely to the generous donations of collectors who understand the importance of having a good representation of Carr's work in a public art gallery in her hometown.

The exhibition and publication *Emily Carr: On the Edge of Nowhere* outlines Carr's career, which was very consciously set in Victoria, in a landscape she loved, on the western edge of Canada. Curator Mary Jo Hughes deftly tells the story of the artist through works drawn, for the most part, from the AGGV collection. Augmenting various aspects of the exhibition are significant loans from the Royal BC Museum, the BC Archives, the Vancouver Art Gallery, the Art Gallery of Hamilton, the Sisters of St. Ann, and Museum London. I thank these lenders for their cooperative support, enabling us to bring to the public a survey of Carr's contribution to modern Canadian art. I am also grateful for the expertise offered by staff of the AGGV and of the lending institutions, as well as Jan Ross of Emily Carr House and Kerry Mason of the University of Victoria.

Jon Tupper
Director

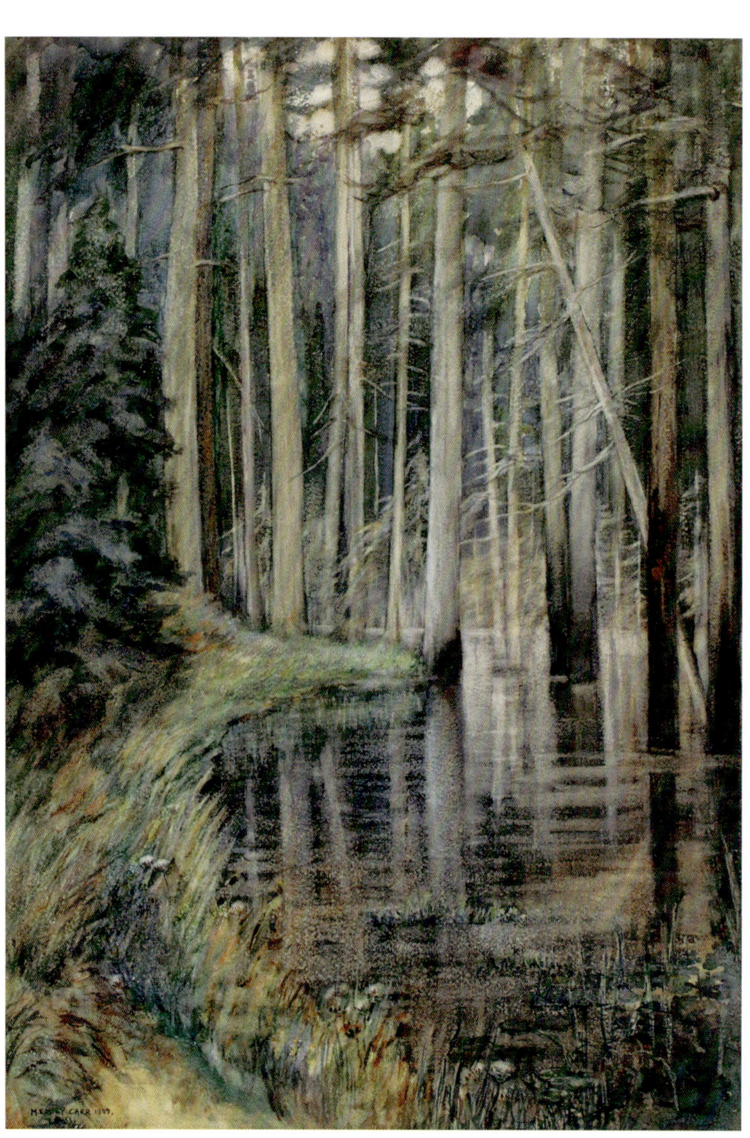

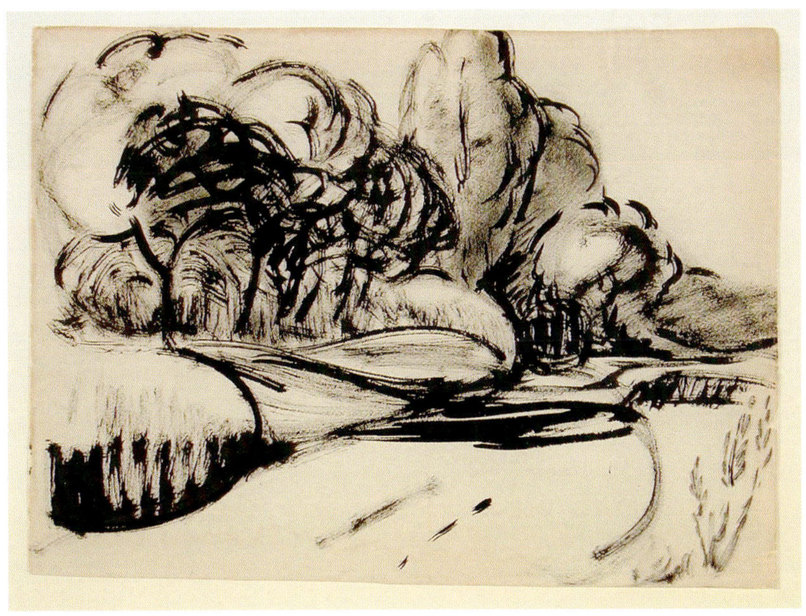

Forest Scene, 1909, watercolour on paper, 54.5 x 37.8 cm, The Art Gallery of Greater Victoria, In memory of Jennet and Louis Davies, Edith and Oswald Parker and James R. Davies, with thanks to Emily Carr, these works are donated by N.E. Davies, Brian, Bruce and Kevin Davies 2005.026.001

Untitled (Tree Study), 1911, ink on paper, 25.7 x 35.2 cm, The Art Gallery of Greater Victoria, Gift of Mrs. Edna Parnall 1988.010.001

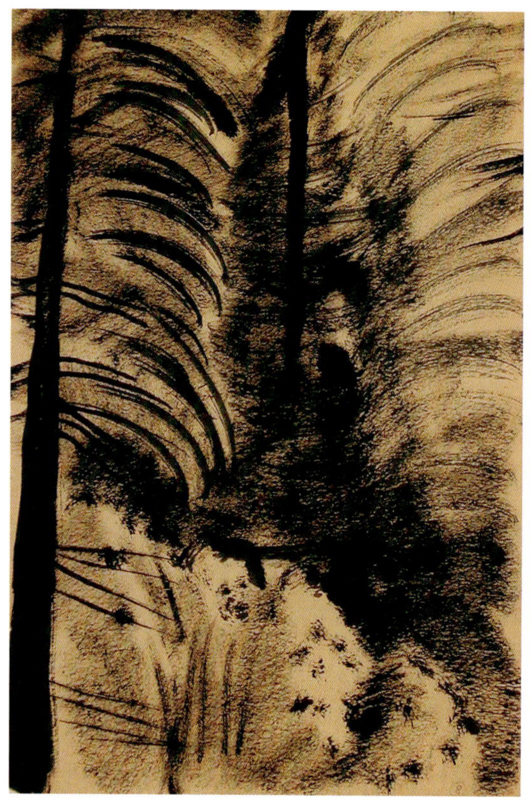

Sketch of Trees, c.1930, oil on paper, 22.5 x 15.1 cm, The Art Gallery of Greater Victoria, Gift of Mr. Peter Ohler 1973.070.001

Blue Sky, 1936, oil on canvas, 93.5 x 65.0 cm, The Art Gallery of Greater Victoria, The Thomas Gardiner Keir Bequest 1994.055.002

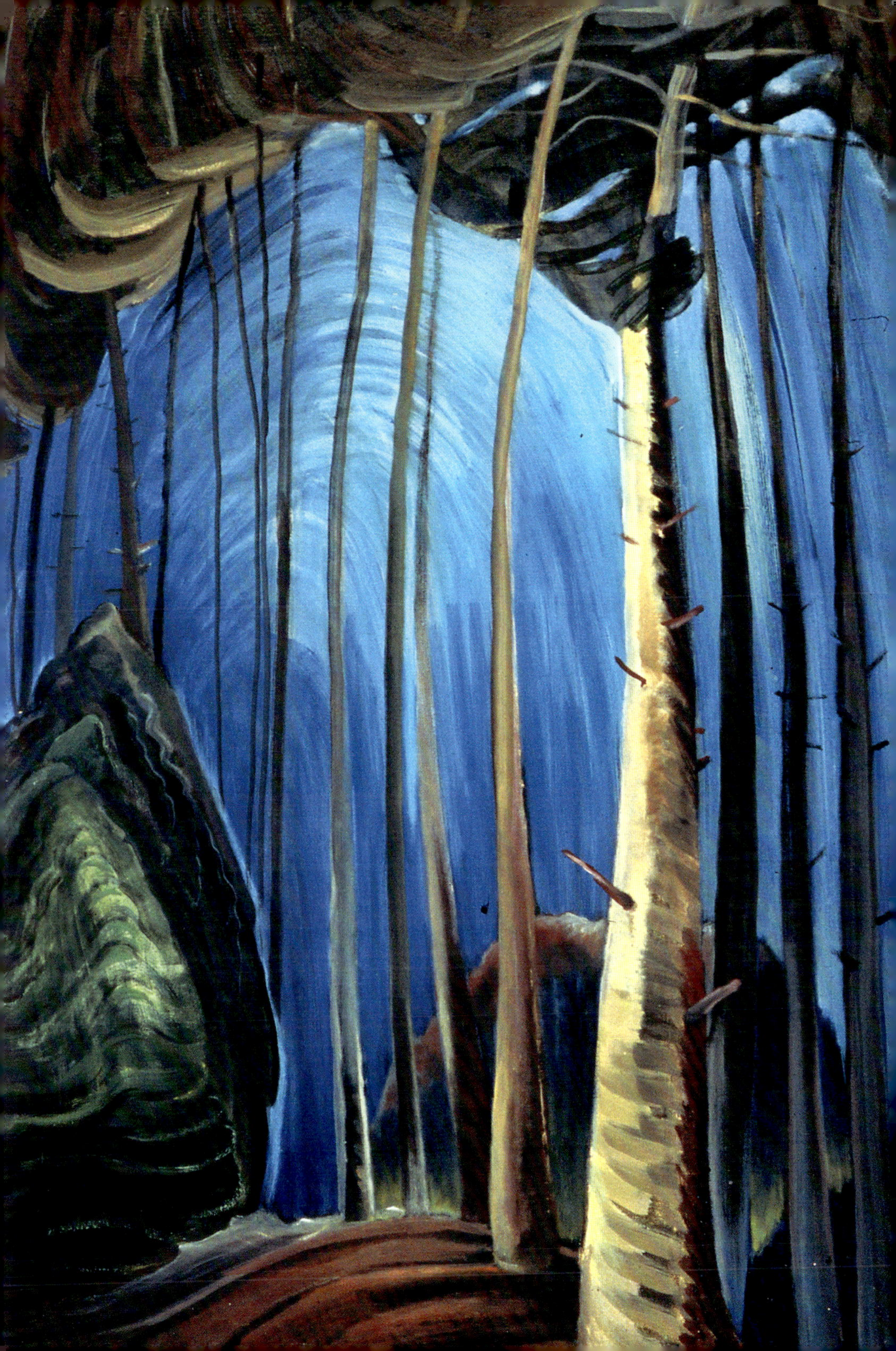

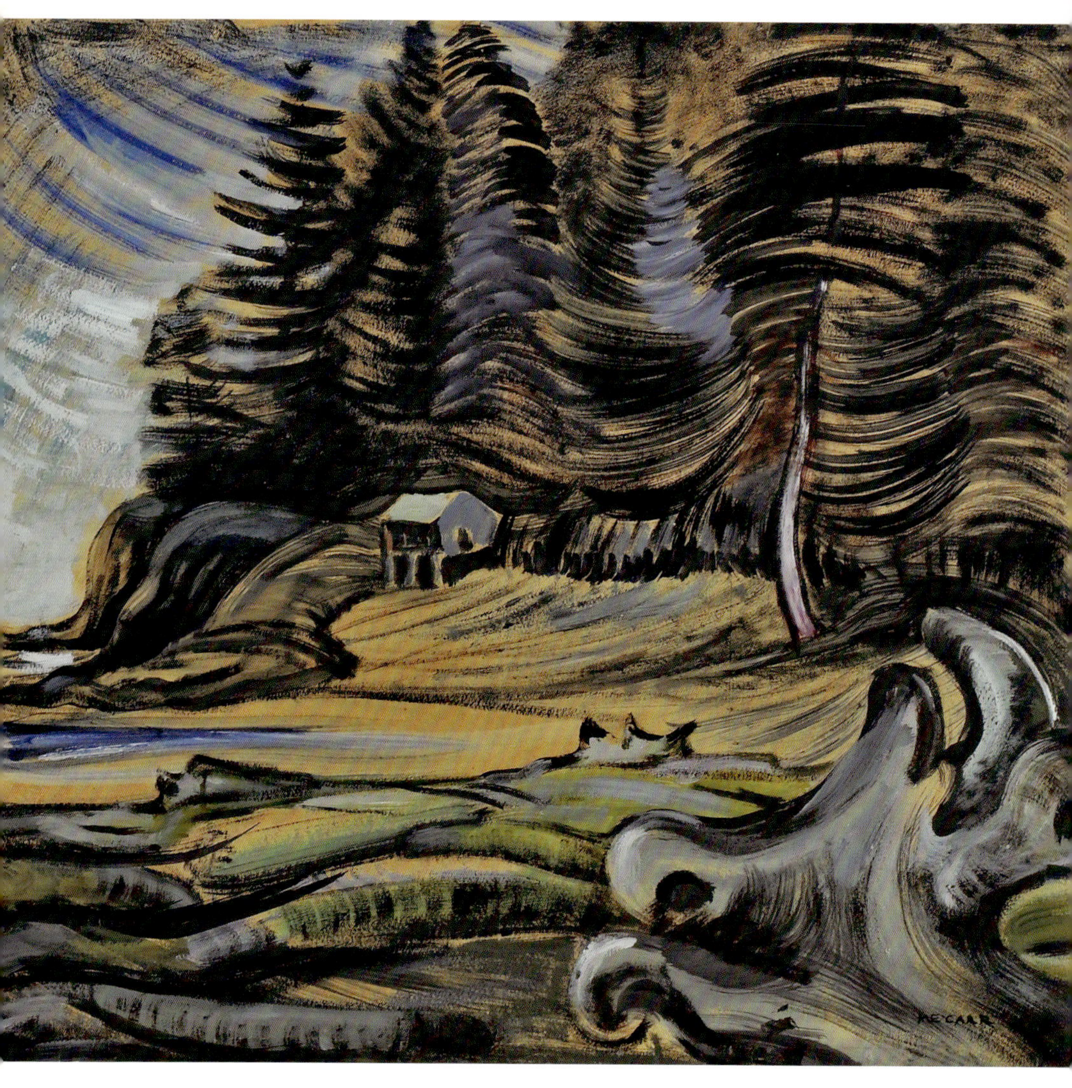

Shore and Forest (Cordova Bay), 1931, oil on paper, 61.0 x 67.9, The Art Gallery of Greater Victoria, Purchased with funds from Mark Tobey 2009.032.001

Emily Carr

On the Edge of Nowhere

MARY JO HUGHES

THAT EMILY CARR DESCRIBED HERSELF AS "a little old woman on the edge of nowhere" is often cited as proof of her low self-confidence and disconnection with the people and movements at the forefront of Canadian art. However, the context in which she said it was ironic: she was poking fun at the National Gallery of Canada when she wrote: "If the work of an isolated little old woman on the edge of nowhere, is too modern for the Canadian National Gallery, it seems it cannot be a very progressive institution."[1] While Carr did indeed harbour feelings of isolation, blaming geography, finances, and her failing health as barriers to her inclusion in what she saw as a burgeoning art scene in the rest of Canada, she overcame these through her determination to grow as a modern artist. Furthermore, her identification as an outsider was belied by the fact that Carr was well-travelled, well-educated, and connected to various cultural figures who supported the realization of her remarkable talent.

Carr triumphed over isolation through her focused drive to contribute significantly to something larger than herself. A significant factor in how she accomplished this was that she took advantage of all that her West Coast location had to offer. While she acknowledged the peripheral location of Victoria, she willingly lived there because she loved it. Indeed, she expressed this sentiment explicitly in her journal when recounting a

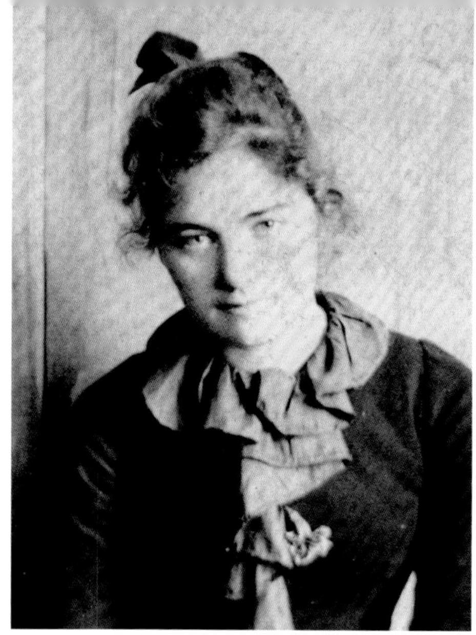

Emily Carr at Age 22, 1893
Unknown Photographer
Courtesy of Royal BC Museum/BC Archives
H-02813

visit from collector Harold Mortimer Lamb:

> *"It's a shame to think of you stuck out here in this corner of the world unnoticed and unknown," says he. "It's exactly where I want to be," says I. And it is, too. This is my country. What I want to express is here and I love it. Amen!*[2]

Her deeply-felt spiritual connection with the natural environment and First Nations cultures of Vancouver Island speaks to us even today through her words and paintings. She immersed herself in the people and landscape, and drew upon both for inspiration and subject matter for her painting that, in the first half of the 20th century, represented some of the most groundbreaking work in British Columbia and Canada. For this, Emily Carr remains a figure of influence in Canada, identified as a pioneer of modernism. She was an artist, writer, and mentor to younger artists. We also recognize her as a visionary, one who imagined and called for what could be possible in the sleepy cultural scene of the Victoria of her day.

Carr was born in 1871 to British parents in Victoria, the new provincial capital on the southern tip of Vancouver Island, separated from mainland British Columbia by the Strait of Georgia. Orphaned at age 16, she was largely raised by her elder sister. Although Victoria remained her home base throughout her life, she spent significant time studying art in San Francisco (1890–1893), England (1899–1904), and France (1910–1911).

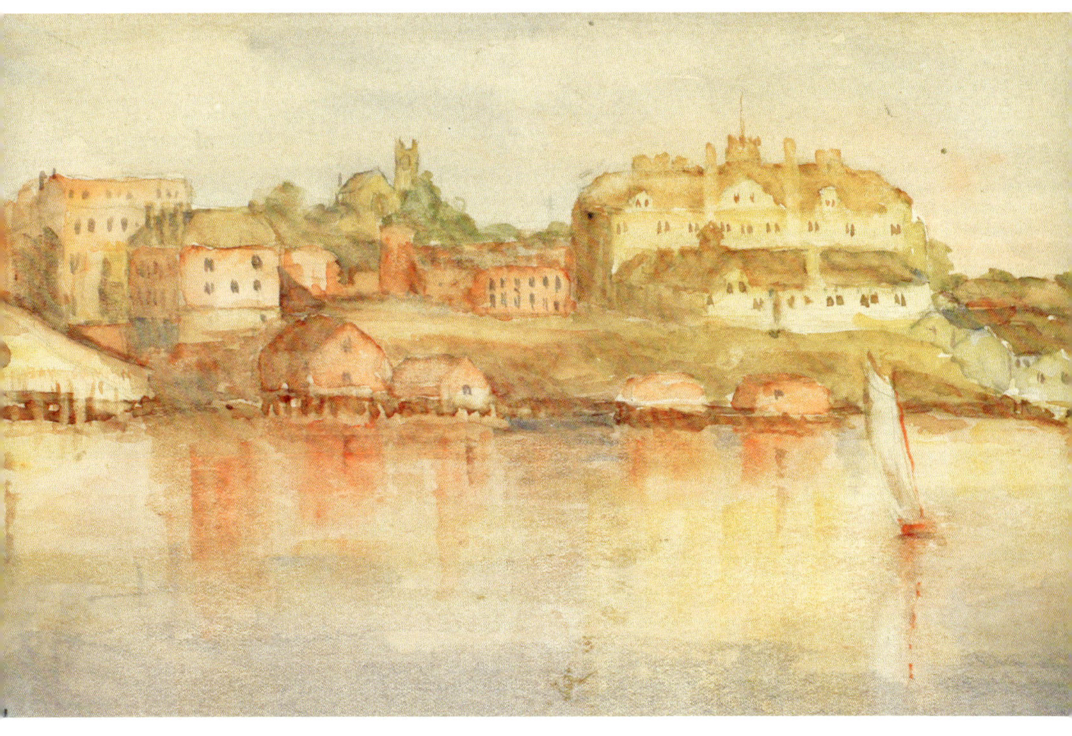

Victoria Inner Harbour, 1905, watercolour on paper, 15.2 x 23.0 cm, The Art Gallery of Greater Victoria, in memory of Jennet and Louis Davies, Edith and Oswald Parker and James R. Davies, with thanks to Emily Carr, these works are donated by N. E. Davies, Brian, Bruce and Kevin Davies 2005.026.003

Her early scenes of Victoria (*Beacon Hill Park*, 1909 and *Victoria Inner Harbour*, 1905) stem from 19th-century British watercolour traditions that she absorbed from childhood art lessons and the traditional training she received in San Francisco and England. Yet even in these works she displayed her love of nature and interest in the power of light, hinting at the commanding mastery of media, technique, and the subject matter that would come to absorb her fully in the painting of her mature years.

Carr looked for new aesthetic and iconographic challenges outside the city when she became discontent with the picturesque and overtly British qualities of Victoria itself. On and off between 1899 and 1933 she visited nearly 50 remote villages, stretching from southern Vancouver Island up the coast into Alaska. Carr was inspired by what she saw and experienced and, as a result, became resolutely wed to a thematic focus on Aboriginal

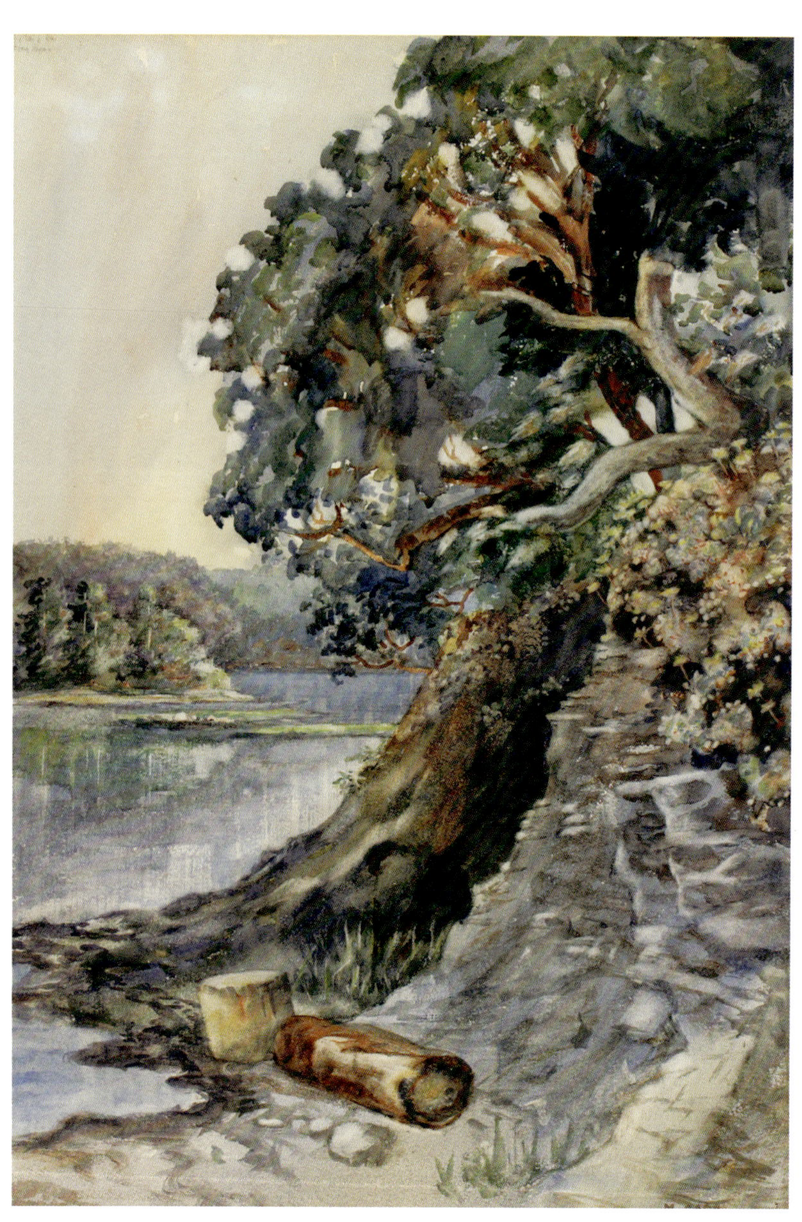

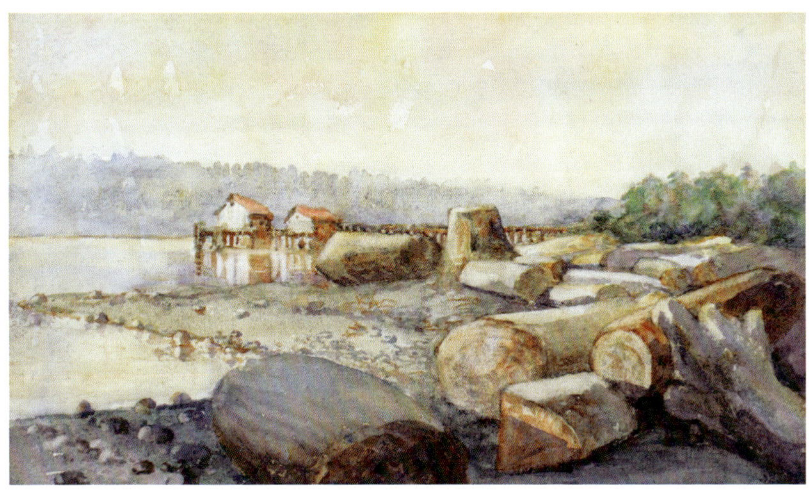

Arbutus Tree, c.1909, watercolour on paper, 54.7 x 38.0 cm, The Art Gallery of Greater Victoria, In memory of Jennet and Louis Davies, Edith and Oswald Parker and James R. Davies, with thanks to Emily Carr, these works are donated by N.E. Davies, Brian, Bruce and Kevin Davies 2005.025.001

Beach Scene with Stumps and Logs, c.1910, watercolour on paper, 16.6 x 27.0 cm The Art Gallery of Greater Victoria, In memory of Jennet and Louis Davies, Edith and Oswald Parker and James R. Davies, with thanks to Emily Carr, these works are donated by N.E. Davies, Brian, Bruce and Kevin Davies 2005.026.002

subjects including villages, people, and totem poles (*Totem Walk at Sitka,* 1907). These works represented a vast departure from what other artists in Victoria were producing at the time. See Kerry Mason's essay for further discussion of the significance of Carr's interactions with First Nations subjects.

While the First Nations work expanded her thinking and subject matter, it was her sojourn in France (1910–1911) that inspired Carr to follow a new way of expressing herself through experimentation with modernist form and colour (*Hillside in France*, 1911). Under the influence of her teacher Harry Gibb, she was convinced that "the 'New Art' was going to help my work out west, show me a bigger way of approach."[3] Following her studies and first-hand exposure to the paintings of European Post-Impressionists, Carr's art revealed a new freedom of colour, line, and spatial relationships

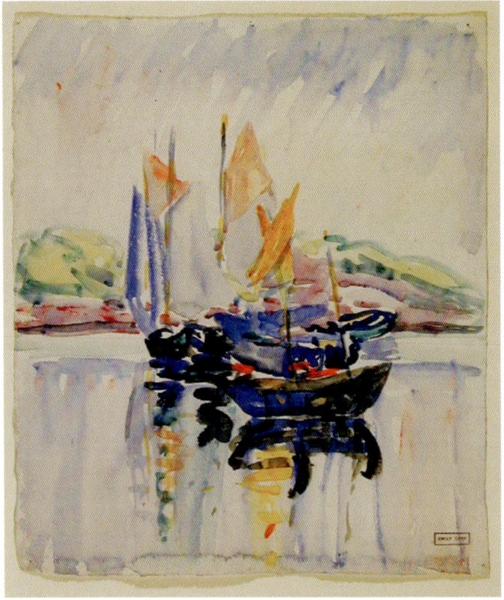

Brittany Coast, 1911
watercolour on paper
29.5 x 26.1 cm
The Art Gallery of Greater Victoria, Gift of Major H.C. Holmes 1964.073.001

Untitled (Hillside in France), 1911, oil on board
23.1 x 18.3 cm
The Art Gallery of Greater Victoria, Flora Hamilton Burns Bequest 1989.037.001

that allowed her to revisit Aboriginal subjects with elements adopted from Fauve and Cubist sources *(Big Eagle (Great Eagle), Skidegate*, 1929):

> *I came home from France stronger in body, in thinking, and in work.... My seeing had broadened. I was better equipped both for teaching and study because of my year and a half in France, but still mystified, baffled as to how to tackle our big West.*

However, her new approach was not readily accepted in Victoria or even Vancouver:

> *I visited in Victoria, saw that it was an impossible field for my work; then I went to Vancouver and opened a studio, first giving an exhibition of the work I had done in France.*
>
> *People came, lifted their eyes to the walls – laughed!*
>
> *"You always were one for joking – this is small children's work! Where is your own?" they said.*
>
> *"This is my own work – the new way."*[4]

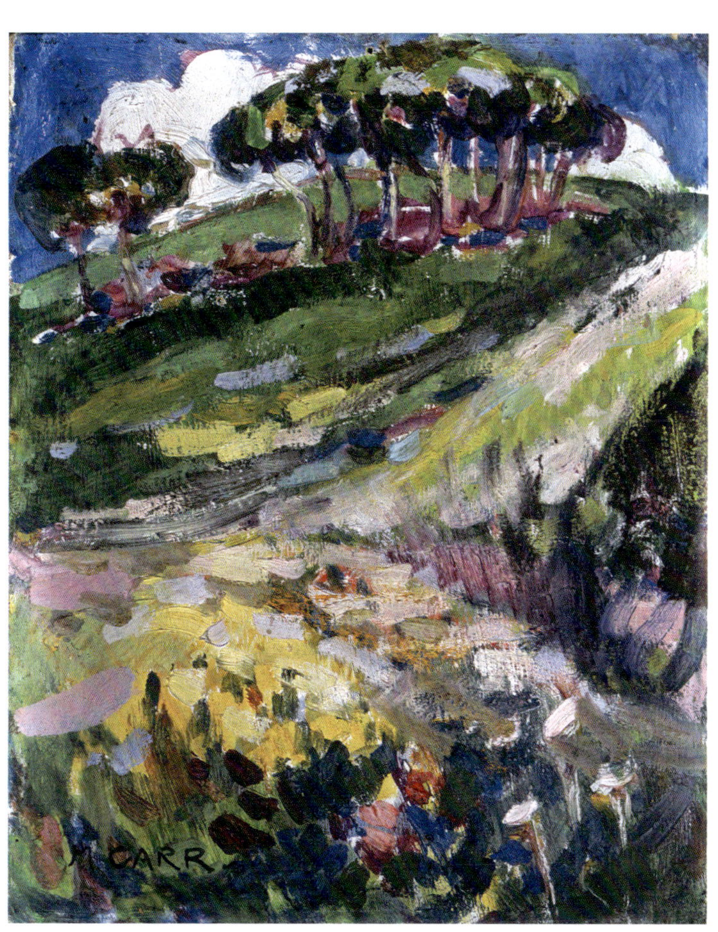
M CARR

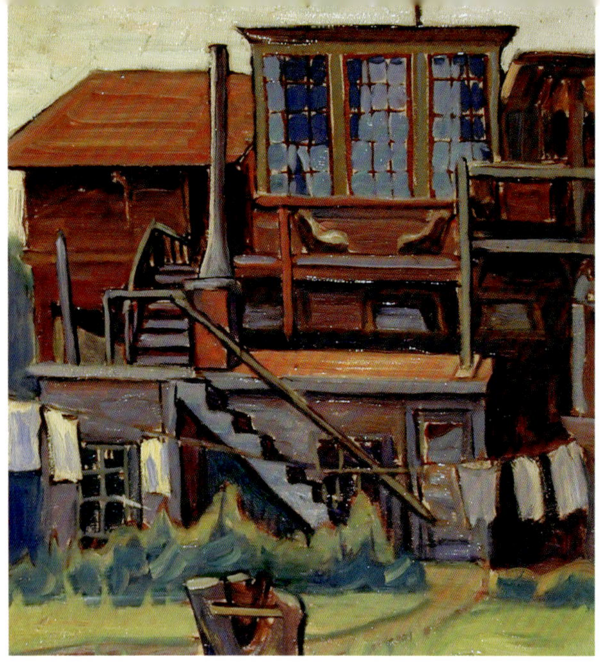

Nan Lawson Cheney
The Back of the House of All Sorts, 1930
Oil on panel
The Art Gallery of Greater Victoria, Gift of the Artist in Memory of Miss Mary Raymur Lawson MBE 1966.020.001

Despite these proclamations that Carr sometimes embellished in her writings, she did sell some of her new work, had supportive artist friends in Vancouver, and even received favourable reviews in the newspaper. However, when she tried to sell these new totem paintings as a cohesive group to the British Columbia provincial government as visual records of what she understood to be a dying culture, she was told they were not documentary enough and too modern. While she pursued painting sporadically when possible over the next several years (1916–1927), other more potentially lucrative activities consumed much of her energies as she struggled to support herself during challenging economic times. These activities included producing hooked rugs and pottery (see illustrations of Klee Wyck pottery) for the tourist trade and functioning as a landlady in her house which she later wrote about in her book *The House of All Sorts*.

In 1927, her work rose to the fore again when the director of the National Gallery of Canada, Eric Brown, and ethnologist Marius Barbeau invited her to exhibit her First Nations subjects in Ottawa in an exhibition of West Coast art. During this trip East she met many other Canadian artists including the well-known Group of Seven. The injection of life that she saw in the Group's paintings (particularly those of Lawren Harris, A.Y. Jackson, Frederick Varley, and Arthur Lismer) reinvigorated and inspired her desire to contribute to a Canadian art revolution. Of this she wrote: "They are

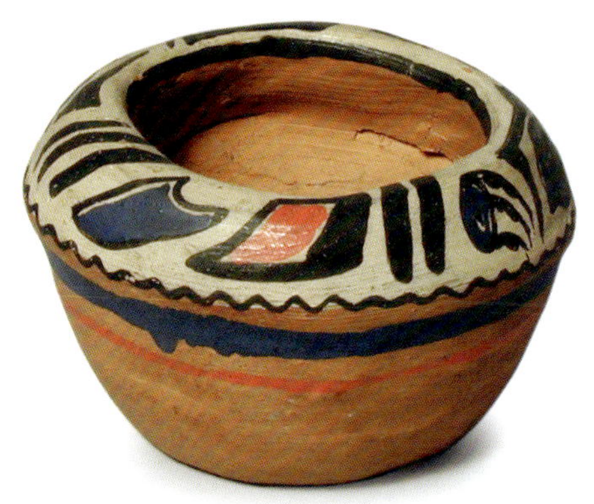

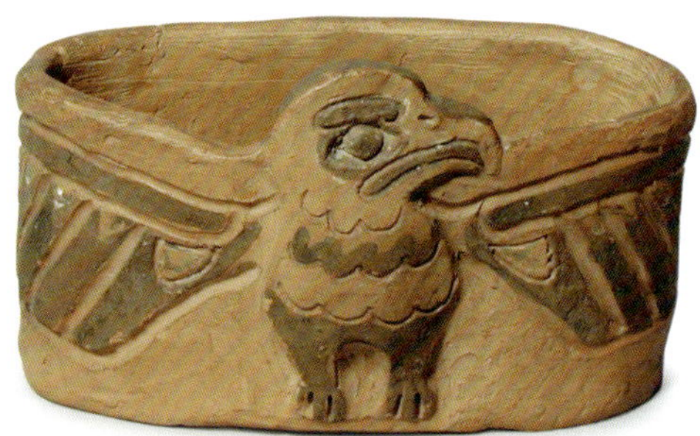

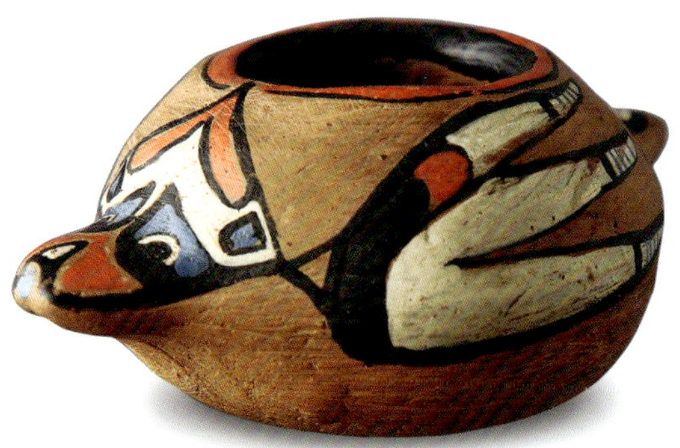

Klee Wyck Bowl, 1924-1930, clay and paint, The Art Gallery of Greater Victoria
4.7 x 8.0 cm, Gift of Commander & Mrs. A.J. Tullis 1973.077.001
6.1 x 6.0 cm, Gift of Humphrey Toms, 1981.026.002
4.7 x 8.0 x 11.0 cm, Gift of Ruth Squire 2009.018.001

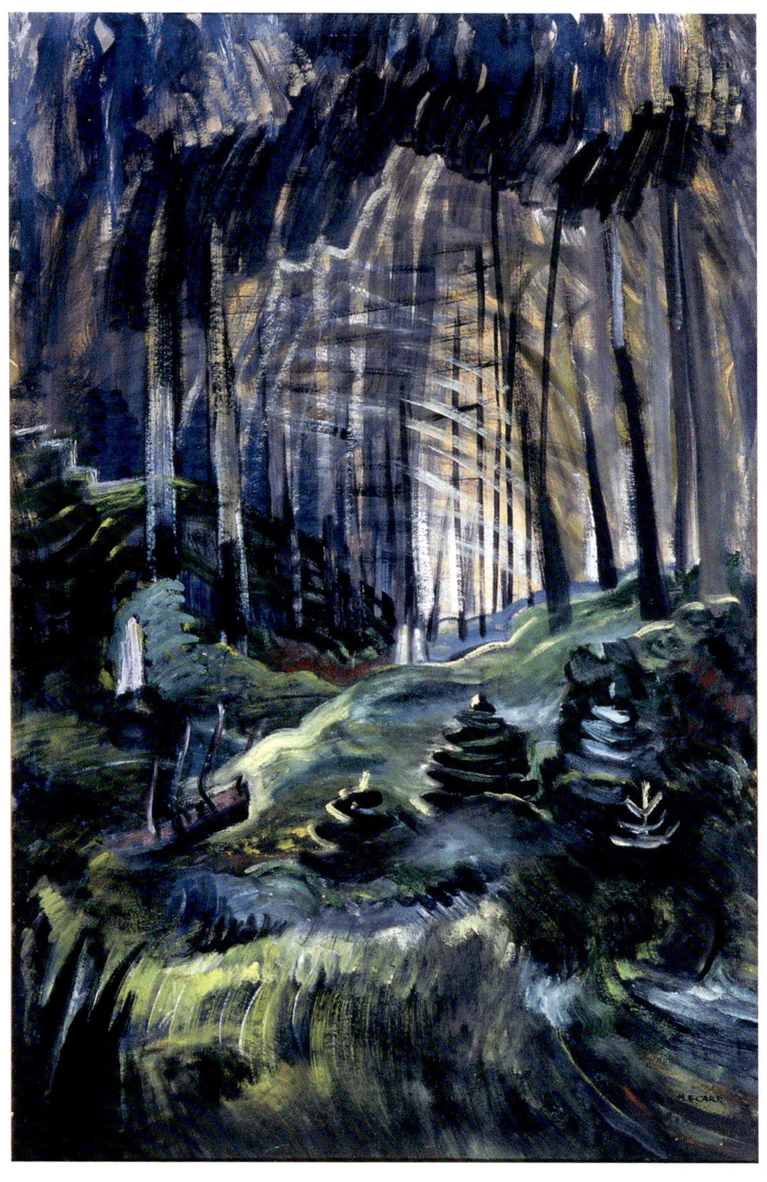

Deep Woods, 1936, oil on paper, 89.6 x 59.6 cm, The Art Gallery of Greater Victoria, Gift of Flora Hamilton Burns and Patricia Keir in memory of their parents, Mr. and Mrs. Gavin Hamilton Burns 1994.055.005

big and courageous. I know they are building an art worthy of our great country, and I want to have my share, to put in a little spoke for the West, one woman holding up my end."[5]

After visiting the studio of Lawren Harris, Emily Carr wrote in her journal:

> *Oh, God, what have I seen? Where have I been? Something has spoken to the very soul of me, wonderful, mighty, not of this world. Chords way down in my being have been touched. Dumb notes have struck chords of wonderful tone. Something has called out of somewhere. Something in me is trying to answer.*
>
> *It is surging through my whole being, the wonder of it all, like a great river rushing on, dark and turbulent, and rushing and irresistible, carrying me away on its wild swirl like a helpless little bundle of wreckage.*[6]

She maintained a significant correspondence with Harris, who more than the others of the Group excited Emily Carr. His support and criticism contributed to Carr's newly found confidence and desire to strike out in new directions in the 1930s. She developed her own repertoire of personal subjects that were particular to her unique experience of the West Coast region of Canada. These included the rain forest, mountains, and ocean-swept skies—subjects that helped her express her spiritual connection to nature and a painting approach that enabled her to create some of the most progressive art in British Columbia at that time.

Another important artistic inspiration was American Modernist artist Mark Tobey. Tobey was an abstract painter influenced by Eastern religions and philosophy. In September 1928, Carr invited him to come from Seattle to teach a master class in her studio. Working with him for three weeks, Carr felt an invigoration that inspired her to explore her inner feelings through form and colour. She wrote to Eric Brown: "I felt I got a tremendous lot of help from his criticisms."[7] While there is no denying that Tobey encouraged her more adventurous explorations of themes beyond totems, it is hard to accept Tobey's proprietary statement:

> *...there would have been no Emily Carr if it hadn't been for me. It is simply not possible that a woman living her circumscribed life could*

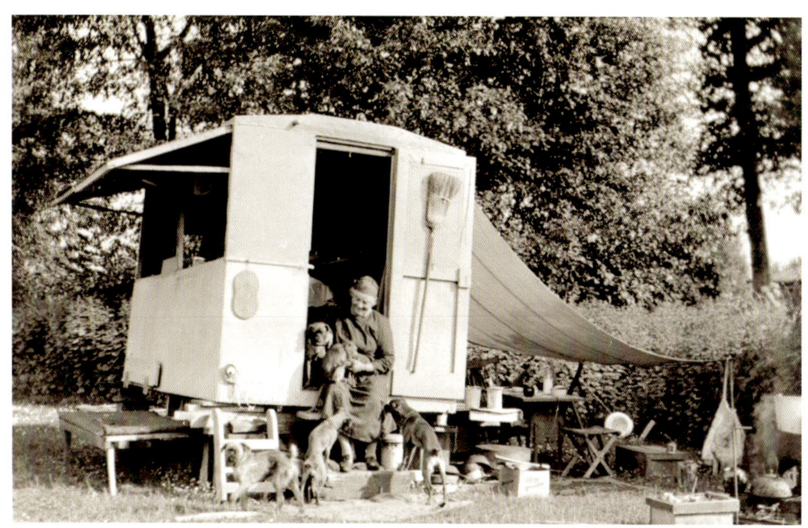

Emily Carr and her caravan "Elephant" at the southwest end of Esquimalt Lagoon,
May 1934, Photo by Mrs. S.F. Morley, Courtesy of Royal BC Museum/BC Archives D-03844

Pine Trees & Blue Sky, c.1935, oil on paper, 91.4 x 60.9 cm, The Art Gallery of Greater Victoria, Gift of Mrs. Joanna McGreevy & Mr. H. Hume Wright 1983.074.001

> *have developed as she did, to conceive the great swirling canvases, the wonderful tree forms, unless there had been someone to indicate the way for her: I was that someone.*[8]

Such public pronouncements continue to propagate "the old woman on the edge" characterization of Carr. They promote an impression that she only had limited access to the outside world and that all she did before Tobey was of little consequence. By the time she met Harris and Tobey she was in her late fifties and had already had years of training and experience. While these men were certainly inspirations to Carr, what is most significant about their encouragement is that it was timely, coming when she was ready to put into practice all that she had experienced.

In works from the last decade of her life we see Emily Carr painting like no other artist of the time. Her statement, *"I am painting on my own vision now, thinking of no one else's approach, trying to express my own reactions,"*[9]

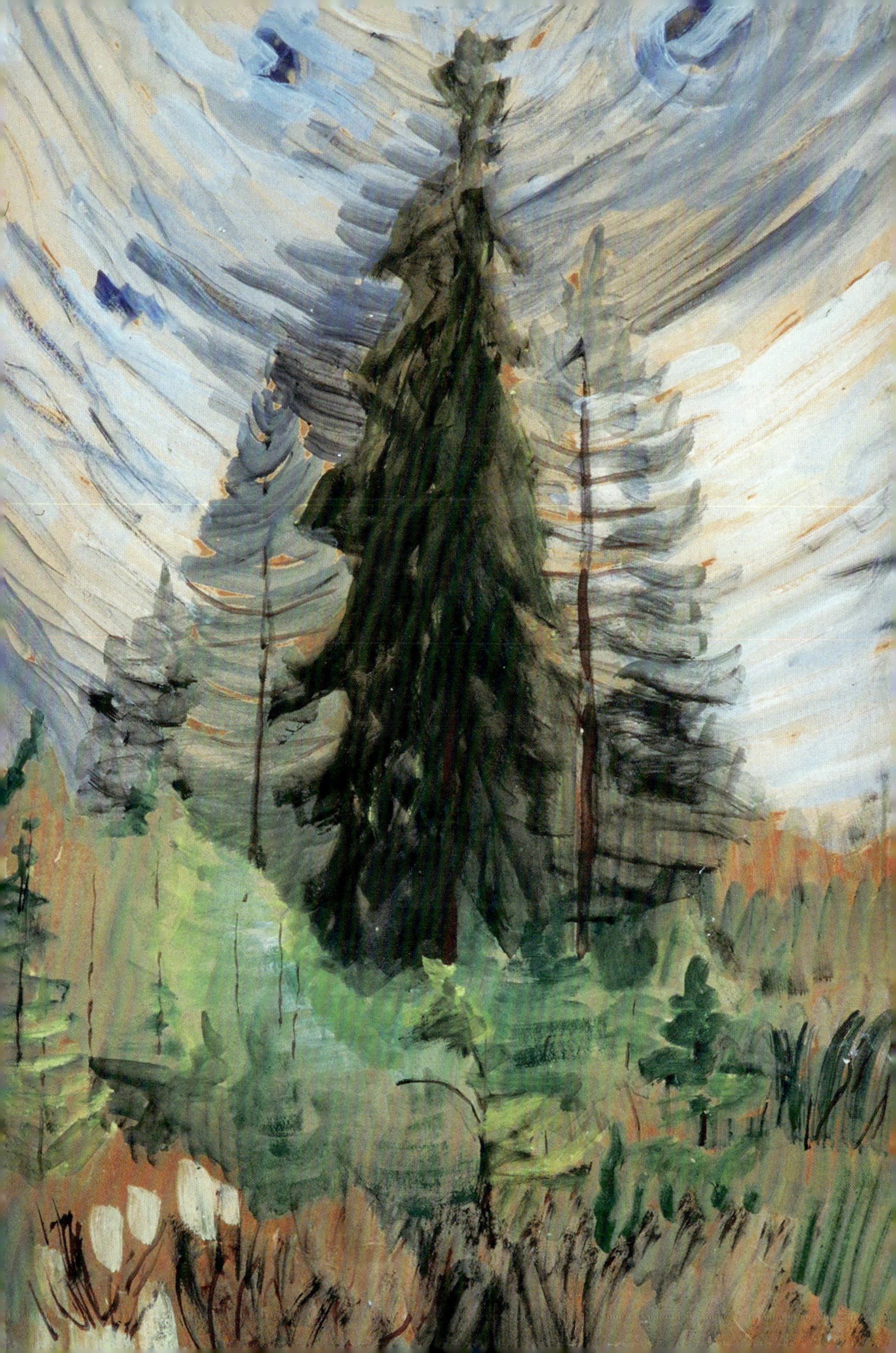

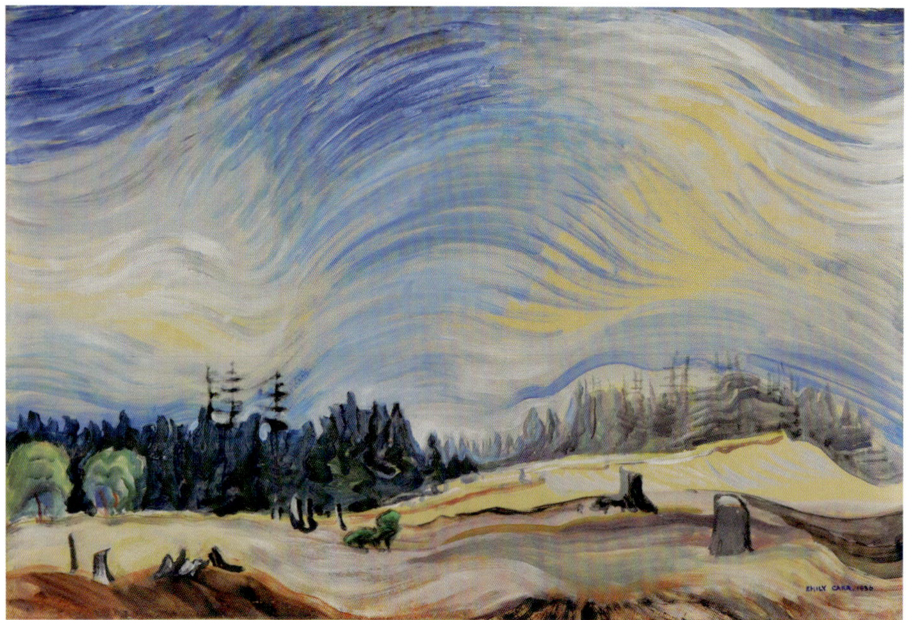

Above the Gravel Pit, 1936, oil on paper, 61.0 x 91.1 cm, The Art Gallery of Greater Victoria, Anonymous Gift 1980.038.001

is borne out today by the fact that there is no mistaking her paintings for any of her contemporaries.

With a new vision in mind to express herself through the landscapes of her beloved West, she found inspiration in the rainforest and shorelines near the southern tip of Vancouver Island. As long as her health allowed through the 1930s and early 1940s, she arranged sketching trips into the forest outside Victoria. There she tapped into a communion with nature that she expressed through paint (*Light Swooping Through*, 1938-39). Always accompanied by her animals (varying combinations of dogs, rats, birds, and the famous monkey named Woo), Emily sometimes spent weeks in the field in the Elephant, a caravan she had retrofitted for sleeping and art making.

In such works as *Juice of Life*, 1938-39 and *Above the Gravel Pit*, 1936, inspired by her trips to Goldstream Park and Metchosin, Carr developed an explosive all-over gestural energy that is spontaneous and direct in its expression of her spiritual connection to her surroundings. These works, although extremely personal, speak of a universal human need to connect with nature:

> *Every day I long for the woods more, to get away and commune with things. Oh, Spring! I want to go out and feel you and get inspiration.*[10]

On a sketching trip in 1935, at Albert Head in Esquimalt, the weather was miserable; as she huddled in the Elephant, Carr wrote down an articulation of the interrelationship of her spiritual and artistic goals:

> *I figure that a picture equals a movement in space. Pictures have swerved too much toward design and decoration. These have their place, too, in a picture but there must be more. The idea must run through the whole, the story that arrested you and urged the desire to express it, the story that God told you through that combination of growth. The picture side of the thing is the relationship of the objects to each other in one concerted movement, so the whole thing gets up and goes, lifting the looker with it, sky, sea, trees affecting each other.*[11]

Indeed, it is her own synthesis of her spiritual beliefs and artistic expressions that bring such authentic feeling to her later works. While they are groundbreaking for their time in terms of their modernist formal qualities, it is indeed the mixture of her personal expressions of her physical and psychic relationship to the West Coast that enables Carr's art to speak to us even today.

That Emily Carr never became complacent is another reason why she still has the ability to captivate us. Right to the end of her life she consistently pushed her art further towards finding true, unique, and meaningful personal expression that spoke not only of her as an individual, but shared her experience of this particular geographical and social landscape. She wrote of this continued ambition as she approached her 65th birthday:

> *I think I have gone further this year, have lifted a little. I see things a little more as a whole, a little more complete. I am always watching for fear of getting feeble and passé in my work. I don't want to trickle out. I want to pour till the pail is empty, the last bit going out in a gush, not drops.*[12]

Even as her health failed she produced fresh work, exhibited more frequently with yearly solo exhibitions at the Vancouver Art Gallery, and tried new things including taking a writing course. Eventually she published several books and, in 1941 at age 70, won the Governor General's Award for non-fiction for *Klee Wyck*, her account of her travels in First Nations communities.

Her interaction with younger artists also sustained her renewed energy later in life. Throughout her career she had taught art classes in both Vancouver and Victoria, thriving on the enthusiasm of her students. As a mature artist, Carr was a significant inspiration to numerous young professional artists. She developed great friendships and, through these, found connections to a more progressive art community than she experienced with local artists her own age:

> *I haven't one friend of my own age and generation. I wish I had. I don't know if it's my own fault. I haven't a single thing in common with them...None of them like painting and they particularly dislike my kind of painting....I have lots more in common with the young generation, but there you are.*[13]

Jack Shadbolt, Max Maynard, and Ina Uhthoff were three young artists who stood out. With them, Carr helped introduce Modernism to the staid local art scene. Less than half her age, Maynard was excited by Carr's work when he saw it at the 1930 Crystal Garden show in Victoria, stating: "I was bowled over....I'd never been so moved by paintings in my life."[14] Shadbolt, whose importance to Canadian art would increase in the coming decades, was supportive in helping Carr obtain annual solo exhibitions at the Vancouver Art Gallery in her later years. Uhthoff had studied in her native Glasgow and under Mark Tobey in the "master class" in Carr's studio. Immigrating to Victoria in 1926, she looked to Carr as a leader in

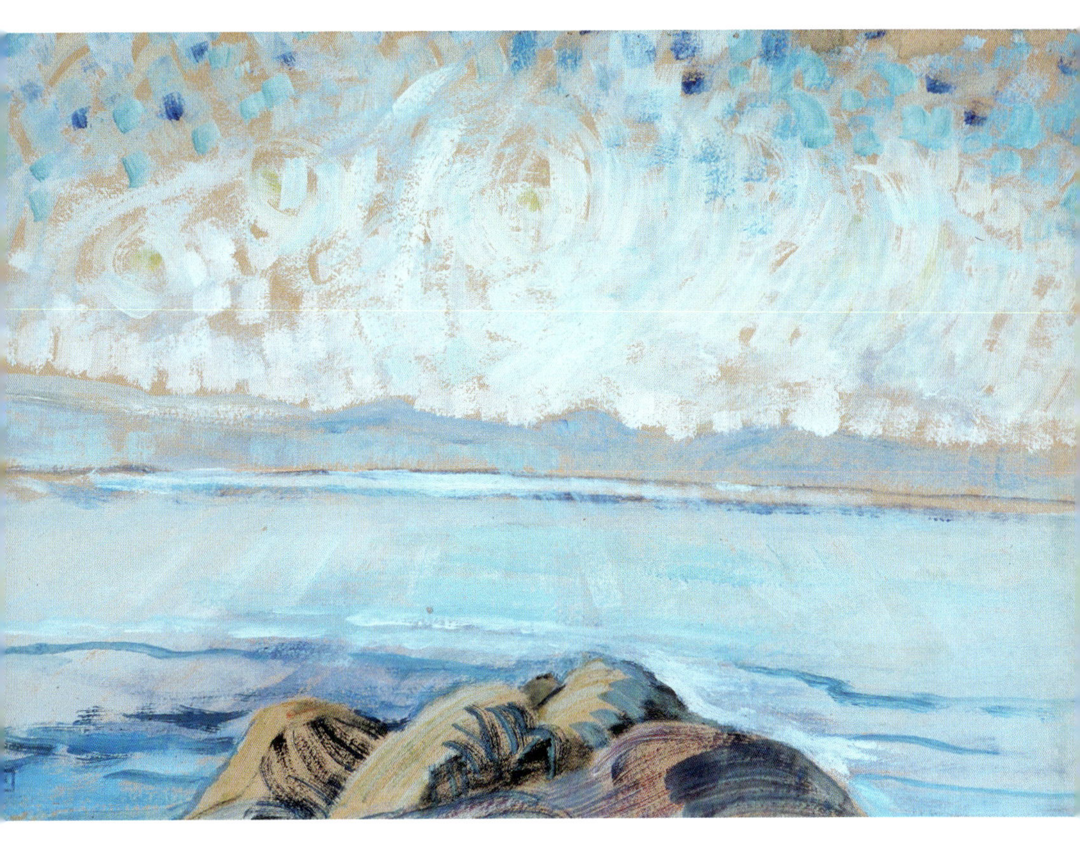

Untitled (Seascape), 1935, oil on paper mounted on board, 26.5 x 40.5 cm
The Art Gallery of Greater Victoria, Anonymous Gift 1997.034.001

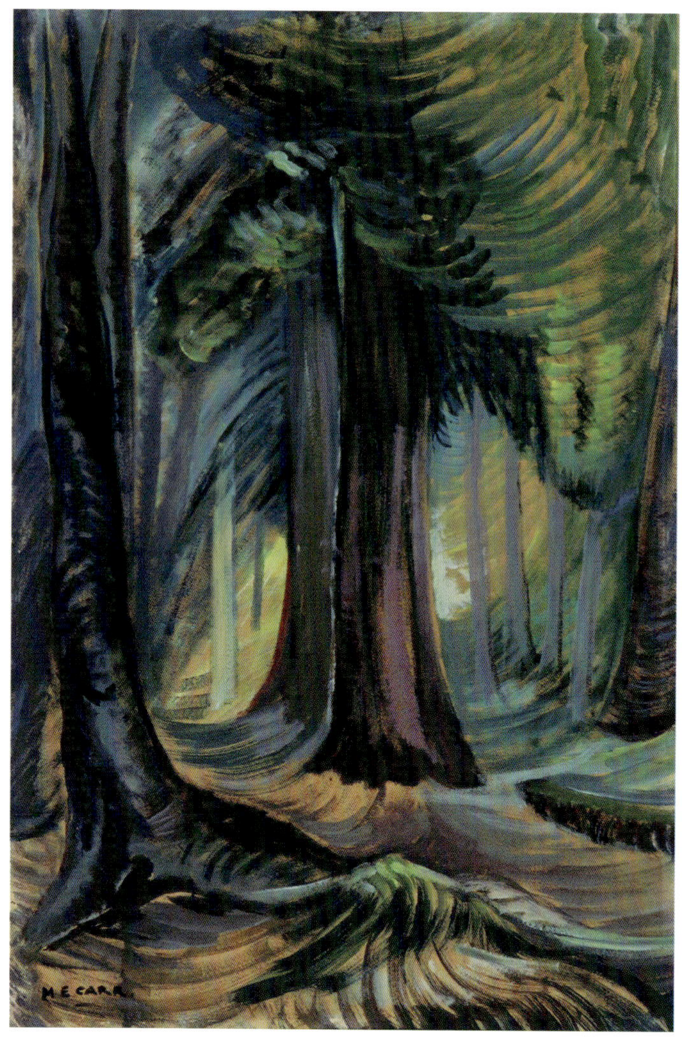

Lone Cedar, 1936, oil on paper mounted on board, 90.8 x 60.1 cm, The Art Gallery of Greater Victoria, The Thomas Gardiner Keir Bequest 1994.055.001

progressive art. Together with Shadbolt, Maynard, Uhthoff, as well as a few others, Carr was instrumental in developing the *Modern Room*, which was a new (and controversial) section of the 1932 Island Arts and Crafts Society annual exhibition. This markedly conservative exhibition was the only art venue available in Victoria at the time. Carr had been consistently frustrated by the venue's backward view of art, and by then she would no longer agree to exhibit in it. The idea of the *Modern Room*, however, enticed her because it allowed artists working in a more modern vein to be presented to the Victoria public. This one-time event was truly the first concerted effort to show modern art in Victoria.[15]

Indeed, another way that Carr promoted modern art in Victoria was through her efforts to establish an art gallery that would stand as a consistent alternative to the Island Arts and Crafts Society exhibition. She was appalled by Victoria's lack of sustained interest in art and had a vision to establish a People's Gallery, a place open to "all classes, all nationalities, all colours."[16] As such, Carr offered her own house as a public gallery and proposed rotating displays of her work and the work of other contemporary artists. In December 1932, she installed the first exhibition and invited the public and dignitaries to hear her speak about the idea. The reactions were decidedly enthusiastic; however, it was the Depression, money was short, and, as a result, there was no available public financial support to keep the gallery running.[17]

However, Carr's passion for sustained culture in her city did not die. It motivated friends and supporters such as Ina Uhthoff to pick up the torch and found the Art Gallery of Greater Victoria a few years after Carr's death.[18] These Gallery founders shared not only Carr's desire to see a permanent home for art in the city, but also her aim for a gallery to be a place where people would see modern art, art that reflected their era. Given Carr's desire to contribute to Canadian art, it is not surprising that her efforts were broadly directed to include painting, literature, and arts advocacy for Victoria, the city she both loved for its beauty and cursed for its conservativism.

ENDNOTES

1 1934 letter to Eric Brown in which Carr complained about the National Gallery of Canada's desire to represent her in its collection by her tamer totem works from 1912–13 rather than her more recent modern work, (NGC, Archives 7.1, Carr, E., 19 October 1934).

2 Emily Carr, *Hundreds and Thousands: The Journals of Emily Carr,* (Vancouver: Douglas and McIntyre) 2006, May 7, 1934.

3 Emily Carr, *Growing Pains: The Autobiography of Emily Carr,* (Toronto: Oxford University Press) 1946, p. 292.

4 *Ibid*, p. 305.

5 Carr, *Hundreds and Thousands*, November 15, 1927.

6 *Ibid*, November 17, 1927.

7 Letter from Carr to Brown, November 1, 1927, National Gallery of Canada as cited in Maria Tippett, *Emily Carr: A Biography*, (Toronto: Oxford University Press) 1979, p. 163.

8 Mark Tobey, *Victoria Times*, March 21, 1957.

9 Carr, *Hundreds and Thousands*, April 24, 1934.

10 *Ibid*, January 18, 1931.

11 *Ibid*, June 12, 1935.

12 *Ibid*, September 23, 1936.

13 *Ibid*, August 12, 1934.

14 Interview with Max Maynard cited in Paula Blanchard, *The Life of Emily Carr*, (Vancouver: Douglas and McIntyre) 1987, p. 221.

15 See Edythe Hembroff-Schleicher, *The Modern Room,* (Victoria, B.C.: Emily Carr Gallery of the Provincial Archives of British Columbia) 1981.

16 Emily Carr, The House of All Sorts, (Toronto: Oxford University Press) 1944, p. 130.

17 In her writings Carr exaggerated the level of disinterest in the People's Gallery: "But influential Victorians were uninterested, apathetic. Why, they asked, was it not sponsored by the Arts and Crafts Society? It was endowed. Unless Victoria could do something bigger and more flamboyant than Vancouver she would do nothing at all." Emily Carr, *The House of All Sorts*, p. 131.

18 See Mary Jo Hughes, *Vision into Reality: Art Gallery of Greater Victoria Early Years, 1951–1973*, (Victoria, B.C.: Art Gallery of Greater Victoria) 2009 for a more thorough discussion of the early years of the Gallery.

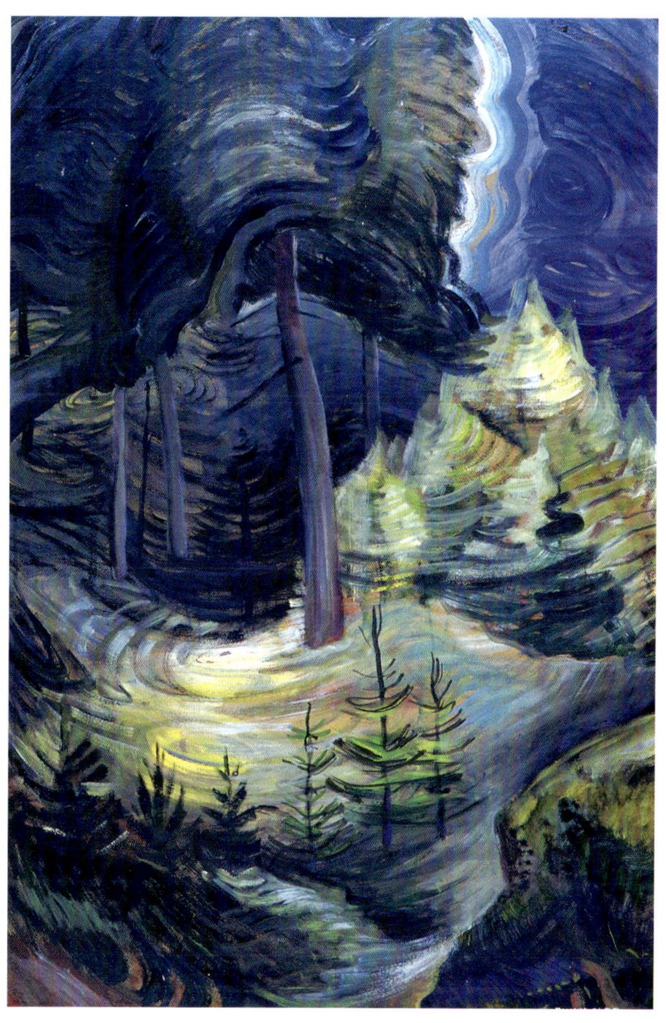

B.C. Forest, c.1938-1939, oil on paper, 87.6 x 56.0 cm, The Art Gallery of Greater Victoria, Ruth Humphrey Estate 1984.050.002

NEXT SPREAD:
Tree, 1935, oil on paper, 81.3 x 101.4 cm, The Art Gallery of Greater Victoria, Gift of Helen M. Piddington and Helen V. Piddington 2001.017.001

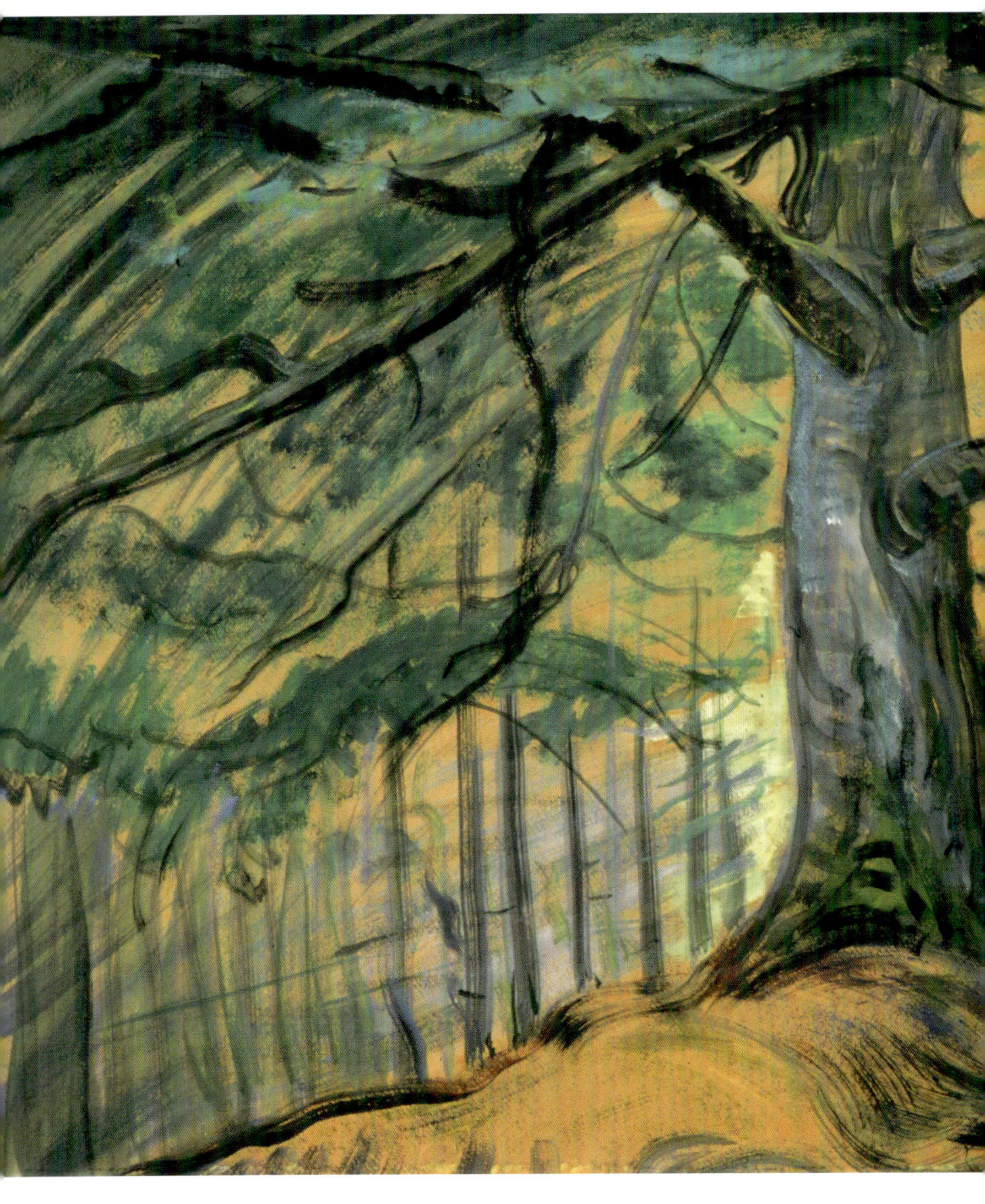

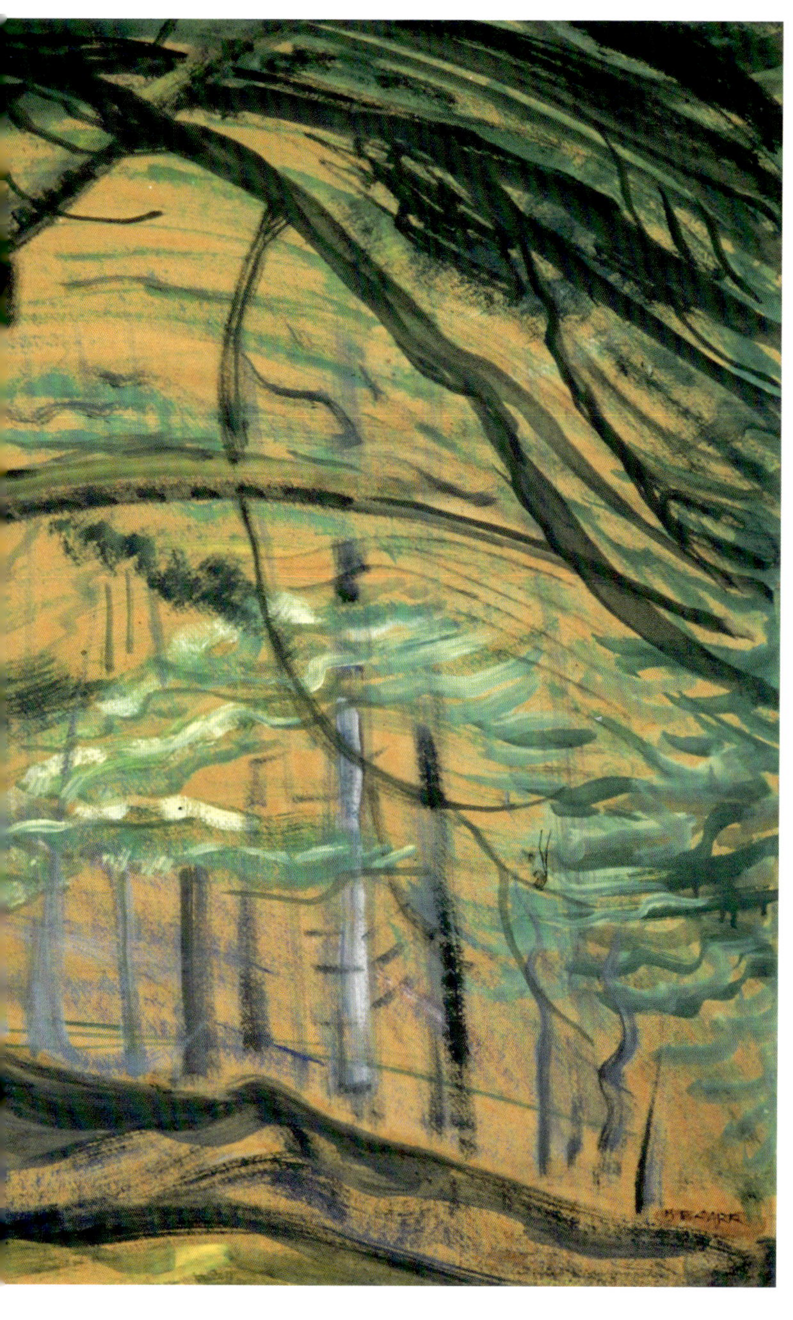

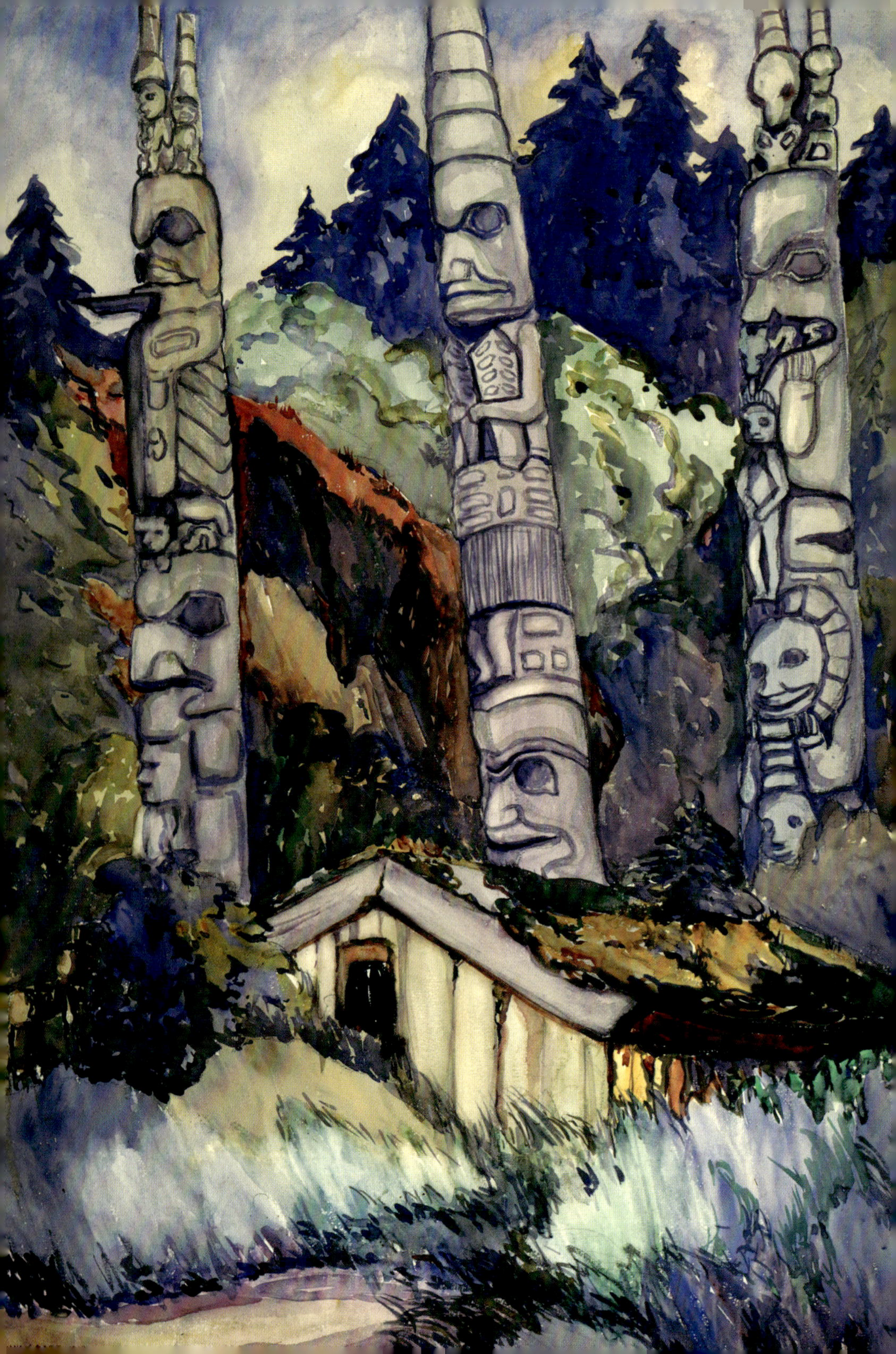

From Wash Mary to Qay'llnaguay

Emily Carr And First Nations

KERRY MASON

IN 1930, LAWREN HARRIS OF THE GROUP OF SEVEN wrote to Emily Carr, "Your work is a joy to us here, a real vital contribution."[1] He referred specifically to the paintings that derived from Carr's second major sketching trip to First Nations villages on the Northwest Coast.

Carr's appreciation, deep interest and affinity for First Nations cultures remained strong from her earliest memories to her final canvases. Her passionate attachment to British Columbia included its First Nations, and her spiritual quest included an understanding of First Nations peoples' relationship with the Northwest Coast environment.

Carr was born in 1871 in Victoria, a city situated on traditional Coast Salish lands. Of British descent, she grew up during Victoria's early development, where the population was two-thirds First Nations.[2] Her earliest memories include watching Songhees people paddling canoes across Victoria's Inner Harbour to her father's provision shop on Wharf Street. The watercolour *Victoria Inner Harbour*, 1905 is the view from the old Songhees (Lekwammen) Reserve where, as an adult, Carr attended a potlatch.[3] In the Carr home, Wash Mary, a Songhees woman who was responsible for the daunting task of caring for the family's laundry, left a positive and indelible impression on

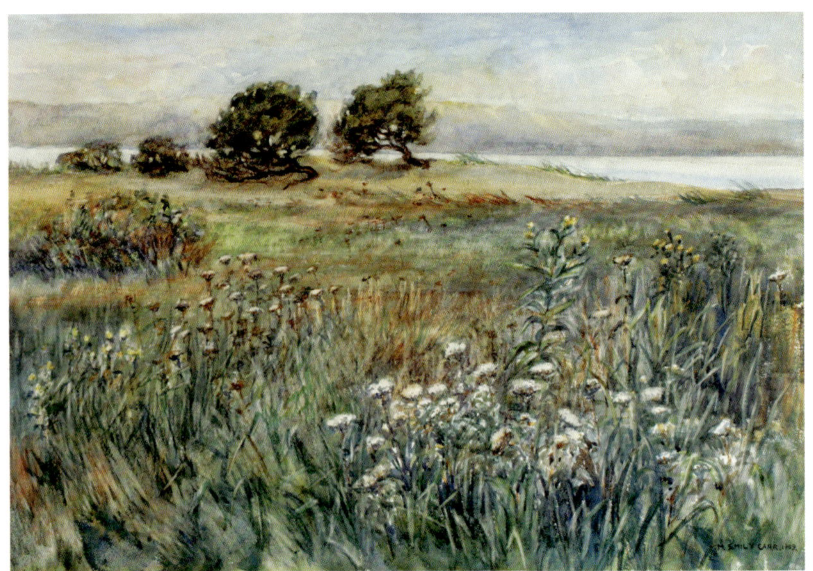

Beacon Hill Park, 1909, watercolour on paper, 35.2 x 51.9 cm, The Art Gallery of Greater Victoria, In memory of Jennet and Louis Davies, Edith and Oswald Parker and James R. Davies, with thanks to Emily Carr, these works are donated by N.E. Davies, Brian, Bruce and Kevin Davies 2005.025.002

PREVIOUS PAGE:
Haida Totem, Cha-atl, Queen Charlotte Islands, 1912, Watercolour on paper British Columbia Archives PDP00612

the young Emily, as did her father's stories of travelling in the 1840s from Chicago to Peru and the indigenous people he met and photographed.[4]

Steps from the Carr family home, Beacon Hill Park was one of Carr's favourite places in the world. Early watercolours, such as *Beacon Hill Park,* 1909, as well as many later oils on canvas and on paper such as *Sea and Sky,* 1933, are interpretations of this coastal parkland. While spectacular geographically, Beacon Hill Park also has significance for First Nations people. The clearing, admired by Sir James Douglas for resembling an English meadow, was the location of camus cultivation for Coast Salish people.[5] On Victoria's beaches, Carr observed First Nations families with their canoes, as the city was a traditional stopping place for their coastal travels from as far away as Haida Gwaii. Growing up in this crossroads fostered in Carr an early and strong attachment to First Nations people.

Carr's first trip to a remote First Nations community was to Ucluelet in 1899. Just weeks before departing for study in England, Carr boarded the steamship the *Willipa* and travelled up the west coast of Vancouver Island, home to the Nuu-Chah-Nulth people.

In pencil, ink, and watercolour Carr recorded the people, houses, canoes, and topography of the community of Ucluelet at the time. Her work is representational, adhering to the traditional 19th century British academic style. It is significant that Carr kept these drawings and paintings in her possession to the end of her life, confirmed by the Emily Carr stamp applied by her estate executors Lawren Harris, Ira Dilworth, and Willie Newcombe.

In Ucluelet, (Etedsu), Emily Carr was given the name Klee Wyck. Linguistically, Klee Wyck is a gerundial construction in the Aht language of Nuu-Chah-Nulth First Nations meaning one who tends to laugh. Not knowing the language, Carr persevered in communicating with the people she met by relying on gestures, dissolving into laughter at her own theatrical interpretations. From this point on, Carr fondly and proudly kept the name Klee Wyck. It would become the title of her first book, a type of pottery she created, a style of rug she made as well as a signature and treasured name. It is a metaphor for the artist's sincere and lifelong appreciation of First Nations people.

In the fall of 1899, Carr travelled to England for a period of study. She brought her Ucluelet sketches to London and even attempted to interest Beatrix Potter's publisher in them. Although they declined, Carr soon found that as a young colonial invited to tea in Belgravia, her Ucluelet experiences were fascinating to others besides herself.

Carr returned home to Victoria at the close of 1904, and then moved to Vancouver where she combined her own painting career with full-time teaching. As time permitted, Carr embarked on sketching trips including a return visit to Ucluelet in 1905. She often visited the Squamish Reserve across Burrard Inlet where her close friend and Coast Salish basket weaver, Sophie Frank, lived. Their friendship, initiated by Carr's purchase of Frank's exquisite baskets, lasted their lifetimes, and it was to Frank that Carr dedicated her award-winning first book *Klee Wyck*. The stories in this book included reminiscences of Ucluelet and more than a dozen other sketching trips to First Nations villages on the Coast. The first edition was illustrated with Carr's portrait of Sophie Frank.

Carr's summer trip to Alaska in 1907 was a pivotal one. Travelling by steamship, en route she visited Alert Bay, Campbell River, and Prince Rupert. The Kwakwaka'wakw culture in Campbell River and Alert Bay had a profound effect on her: "The Indian people and their Art touched me deeply."[6] In Sitka, Alaska, Carr was inspired to paint *Totem Walk at Sitka, 1907*, a collection of Haida and Tlingit poles removed from several villages and re-erected as a tourist site by Alaska's Governor John Brady.[7] Travelling down the Coast, Carr committed to her artistic mission of documenting all she could of what she and others at the time perceived as the "vanishing totems" and way of life of First Nations people:

> My mind was made up. I was going to picture the totem poles in their own village settings, as complete a collection of them as I could. [8]

Time away from teaching in Vancouver was spent in her quest to record First Nations cultures. Carr travelled to the Coast Salish community of Sechelt, recording canoes, houses, people as well as the topography of this coastal settlement. Carr also travelled to Hope, Lytton, Sproat Lake, and Britannia Beach, and returned to Alert Bay in the summers of 1908 and 1909. Several watercolours attest to her fascination with the house and frontal pole of the community's Chief Wawkyas. The distinctive ceremonial front entrance incorporated a recycled Kwakwaka'wakw canoe as the upper beak of Raven. Thunderbird on the top of the pole and the other crest figures of the pole were carefully rendered by Carr:

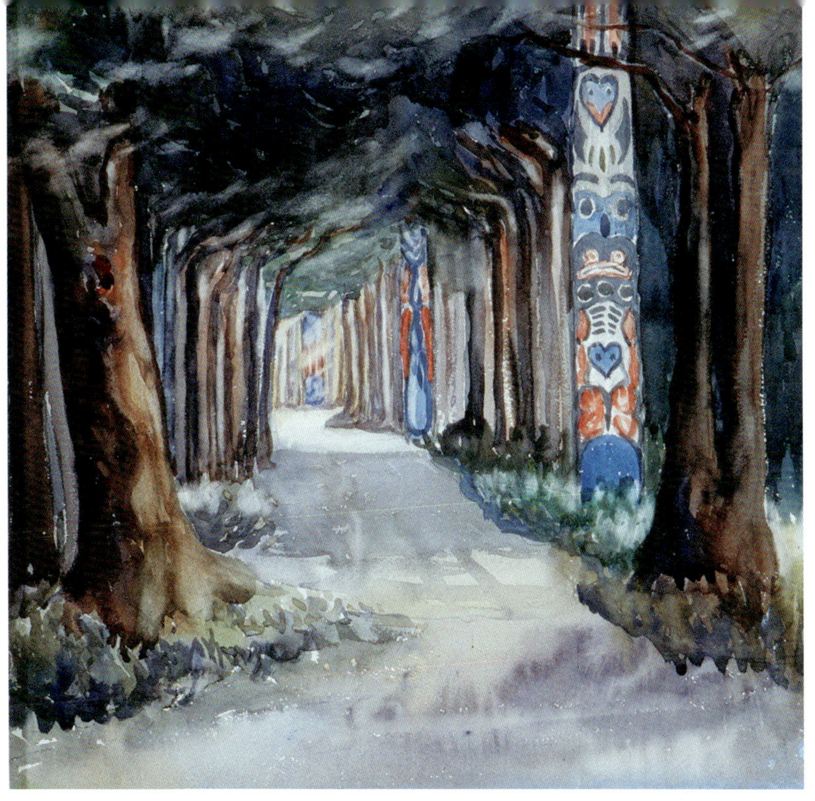

Totem Walk at Sitka, 1907, watercolour on paper, 38.5 x 38.5 cm
The Art Gallery of Greater Victoria, The Thomas Gardiner Keir Bequest 1994.055.004

> You must be absolutely honest and true in the depicting of a totem for meaning is attached to every line.[9]

In 1910, anxious to know about the new art movements that were taking Europe by storm, Emily Carr left for Paris. Carr wanted a fresh new modern approach with which to pursue her First Nations themes. She found it in the Post-Impressionist and Fauve styles during her studies at the Académie Colarossi in Paris and then especially with her teacher, Henry Phelan Gibb, in Crécy en Brie and Brittany. Her final studies in France were watercolour classes in Brittany with Frances Hodgkins. The bold palette, quick brushwork, and spontaneous *en plein air* approach thrilled Carr. Gibb praised her work, especially her colour sense and paint application. He was also enthusiastic about Carr's Ucluelet sketches, which she had brought with her once again to Europe. This approbation for her "Indian Collection"

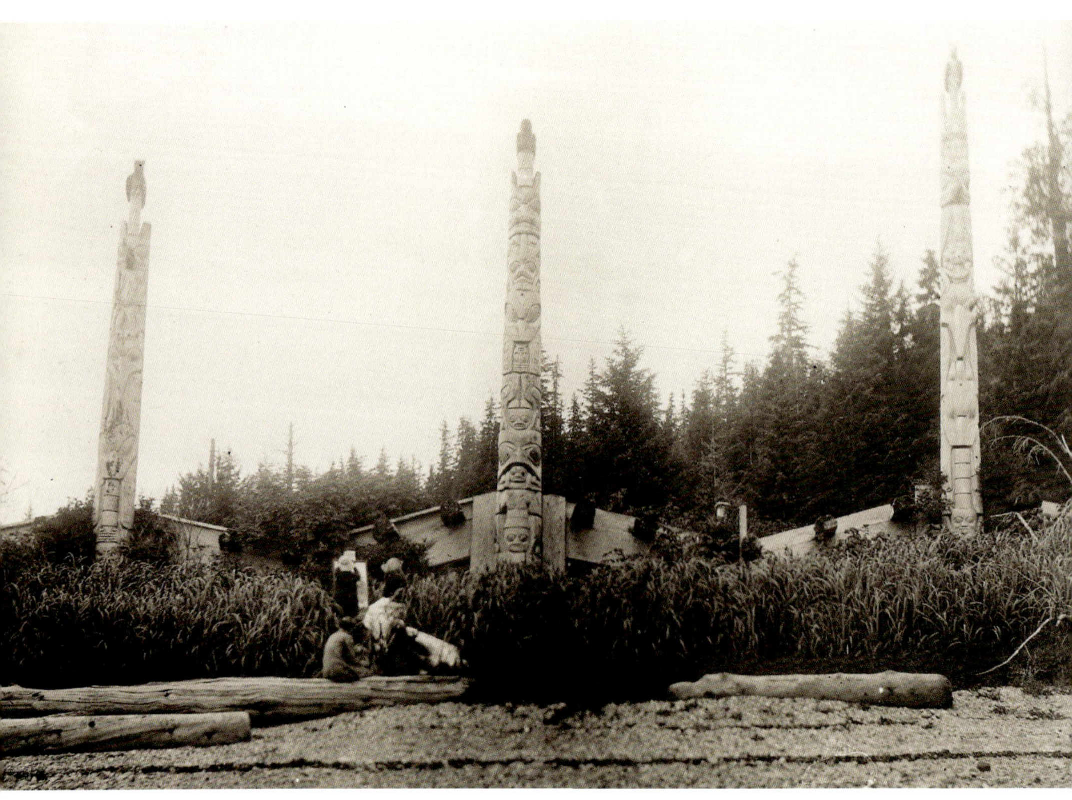

Emily Carr on the beach on Tanoo 1912, Courtesy of Royal BC Museum/BC Archives F-00254

supported her artistic mission. In France, Carr grew out of her conservative representational depictions of her subjects. The new style of painting she was learning was about colour and light, imagination and emotion. Emily Carr embraced it completely and returned to British Columbia at the end of 1911 firmly in the modern camp, expressing her world through colour and form not only as she saw it, but also as she felt it.

In April 1912, she exhibited 70 works with the plan to finance an extensive sketching trip up the Coast. The majority of the reviews of these works were positive, and much of the 1911 and early 1912 works did sell. Significantly, one of the first paintings created in her Vancouver studio in the Post-Impressionist style was an oil on canvas of Ucluelet. Bold blocks of colour and energetic brushwork make this a modern work. The subject matter of the Nuu-Chah-Nulth house, belonging to Cedar Canim, a prominent elder in Ucluelet, makes this the first addition to Carr's "Indian Collection" in her new modern style.

In July 1912, with her favourite sketching partner, her dog Billie, Carr embarked on an ambitious sketching trip, travelling beyond Alert Bay to the remote and, in many cases, abandoned villages of Haida Gwaii, and the Tsimshian and Gitxsan villages on the Skeena River of northern British Columbia.

In Alert Bay she made side trips to neighbouring, yet even more remote, Kwakwaka'wakw villages: Guyasdoms, Mimquimlees, Tsatsisnukomi, and others. From Prince Rupert she boarded the sternwheeler up the Skeena River to the Gitxsan communities of Kispiox, Kitwanga, and Kitseguecla as well as Gitanmax. Carr worked tirelessly, producing a legacy of visual records of these villages before the Totem Pole Preservation Committee of the Federal Government resituated, restored, and removed poles.[10]

Travelling back down the Skeena, Carr crossed Hecate Strait to Haida Gwaii and the village of Masset. From there, she took the five-day steamer tour down the eastern side of the islands to Jedway in the south. Carr extended her trip when she reached Skidegate, hiring William and Clara Russ, a Haida couple from Qay'llnagaay, to take her by boat to the abandoned villages of Cha-Atl, Heina, Cumshewa, Tanu, and Skedans. William and Clara appear in *Klee Wyck*, as Jimmie (with the good boat) and Louisa. Carr also travelled across Masset Inlet to Yan and Ka-Yang by Haida canoe, paddled by a Haida woman with her baby tucked between her knees.

In these villages Emily Carr gathered a wealth of material that would be a recurring focus throughout her prolific career. Carr found that in her recording of totem poles and villages she needed to be as accurate as possible, but once she reworked her sketches in her Vancouver studio over the fall and winter of 1912 and 1913, she was able to give full rein to all she had learned in France, particularly in her treatment of the sky and landscape. In 1913, Carr rented Drummond Hall in Vancouver and presented more than 200 works. These ranged from her Ucluelet sketches and paintings of 1899 and timid watercolours of 1905 to vivid oils and watercolours of 1912 and 1913, such as *Haida Totem, Cha-Atl, Queen Charlotte Islands* resulting from her French training. Her later works are confident paintings, oils composed of thick strokes of rich colour from a loaded brush. Bold composition, assured technique, and vibrant colours characterize Carr's art from the 1912–1913 period.

Carr's work gives us what no historic photographs from 1912 can: colour. In several instances, she provided details of poles that were never photographed. We are indebted to Carr for providing a record of the poles in context. In *Tanoo, Q.C.I.*, 1913, she provides a detailed visual record of three Haida six-beam houses with their frontal poles. When Carr arrived on Tanu Island, the village had been abandoned for two generations: 95 percent of the Southern Haida population had been decimated by waves of disease, principally smallpox.[11] Carr's painting takes on further significance as the next summer these very poles were cut down and removed to be cared for jointly by the University of British Columbia and the British Columbia Provincial Museum.

Carr proposed that the British Columbia provincial government purchase her "Indian Collection" in its entirety for the rumoured new art gallery that would be housed in the Parliament Buildings in Victoria. In 1913, Dr. Charles Newcombe, physician and anthropologist, was solicited for his opinion by the Provincial Secretary. Newcombe advised against it, but did purchase four paintings for himself. This purchase represented the beginning of what would become the largest private collection of Emily Carr works—works that were, ironically, purchased by the B.C. government in 1961 and now form the nucleus of the Royal BC Museum's Carr collection.

Although disheartened, Carr had other grand plans. She had completed her designs for her dream home, with ideal studio space, to be built on her share

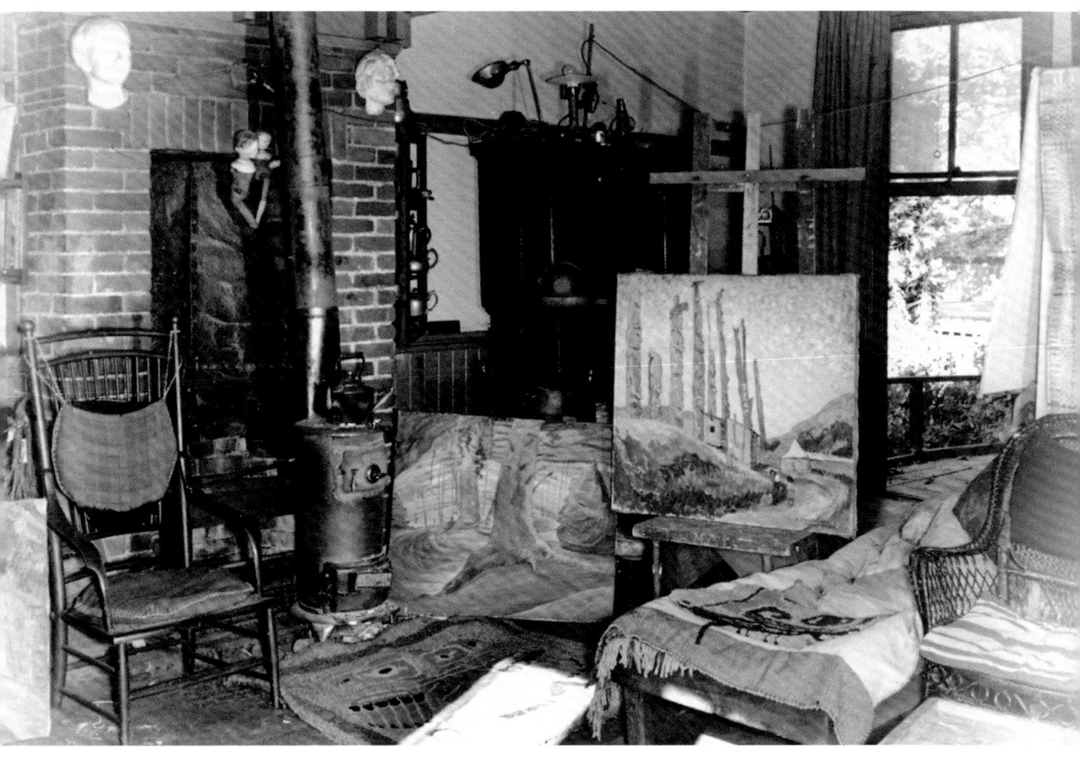

Interior of artist Emily Carr's studio, 218 St. Andrew's St., Victoria, c. 1945
Photo by Ken McAllister, Courtesy of Royal BC Museum/BC Archives E-01422

of the Carr property adjacent to Beacon Hill Park in Victoria. Three rental suites were incorporated to ensure her financial independence, enabling her to paint as she wished. However, Hill House, (later immortalized in *The House of All Sorts*, Carr's third book) soon became the bane of Carr's existence.

In retrospect, Carr called 1913–1926 her barren or bitter years, yet they are illuminated by her energy and creativity. Emily Carr raised more than 350 sheepdogs, ran her apartment house, worked as a cartoonist for *Western Woman's Weekly*, raised rabbits and chickens, grew and sold vegetables and fruit, looked after her own menagerie, wrote stories, hooked rugs, and was a successful potter. She continued to paint and exhibit, especially in

Seattle. When Carr says she "painted little" it's a relative term for this prolific artist. Carr's "Indian Collection" was in hiatus, but not her interest in First Nations culture. Yearning for the First Nations villages which had made an indelible impression on her in 1912, Carr painted two huge Northwest Coast form line eagles and rows of frogs on her attic ceiling:

> Sleeping beneath these two strong birds, the stout western maple tree beneath my window, is it wonder that I should have strong dreams that folded me very close.[12]

Starting in 1915, Carr created hand-hooked rugs from recycled clothing, incorporating references to First Nations crest motifs such as a split eagle. Between 1924 and 1934, Carr created pottery using clay from Beacon Hill Park and firing it in a homemade kiln in her back garden. These hand-formed, hand-painted objects ranged from bowls and bells to candlesticks and lamps. Although her Klee Wyck pottery sold steadily across Canada and she needed this income, Carr felt guilty about using First Nations iconography on pottery, which itself was not an indigenous art form. She hoped it would be understood that she was expressing a love for the cultures of the Coast.[13]

Carr's First Nations work brought her to the attention of the National Gallery of Canada in Ottawa. In 1927, the invitation to participate in the groundbreaking *Exhibition of Canadian West Coast Art: Native and Modern* was a major turning point for Carr.[14] Noted ethnologist, Marius Barbeau, and Eric Brown, Director of the National Gallery, learned of Carr through circuitous routes, involving the support of her friends Sophie Pemberton and Harold Mortimer Lamb. When Brown visited Carr in 1927 it was not her landscapes but her "Indian Collection," complete with Klee Wyck pottery and rugs, that he wanted for this major exhibition. Carr's work had the largest representation of villages from every cultural group on the Northwest Coast. Her compelling modern post impressionistic sketches and paintings of Northwest Coast villages, such as Yan, Kispiox, Hagwilget, Alert Bay, Skedans, and Kitseguecla provided a unique style and context.

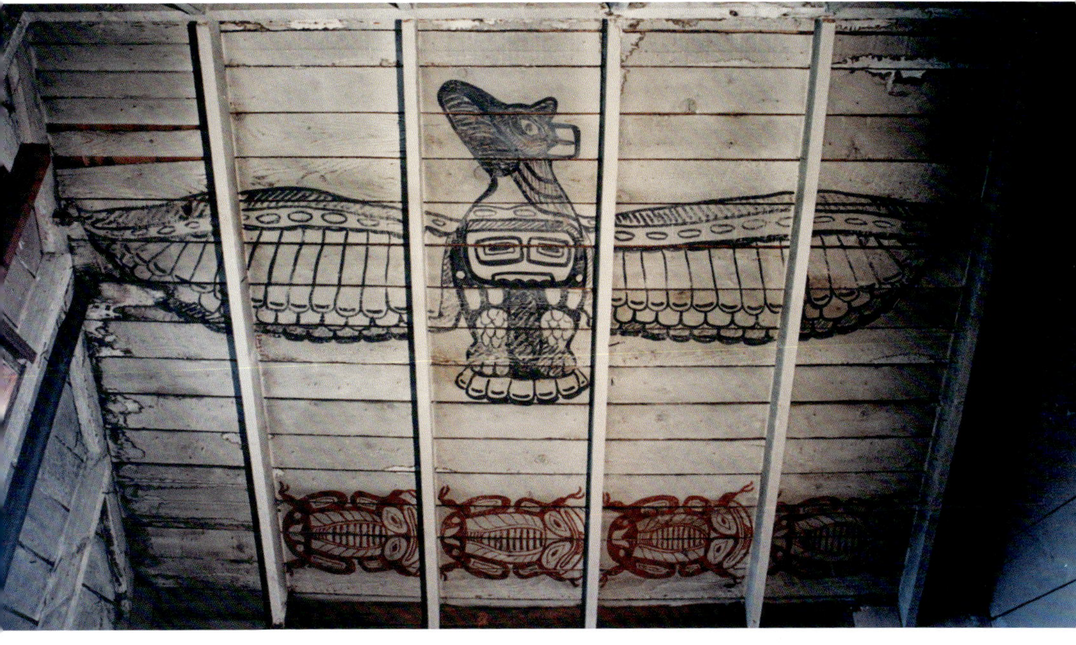

Thunderbird painted by Carr on ceiling of her studio at Hill House (House of All Sorts)
Photograph by Michael Breuer, 1982, Courtesy of Kerry Mason

NEXT PAGE:
Totem and Forest, 1931, oil on canvas, 129.3 x 56.2 cm
Collection of the Vancouver Art Gallery, Emily Carr Trust VAG 42.3.1

Not only had Carr travelled extensively but she recorded the poles in their original sites. Carr also provided key early paintings for the *Exhibition of Canadian West Coast Art: Native and Modern.* She had sketched remote villages long before any of the other modern artists participating in this exhibition did, and even before Marius Barbeau had started his field work in the Skeena. Carr had been painting on the Skeena in 1912; the paintings by A.Y. Jackson and Edwin Holgate resulted from just one brief visit to the Skeena in 1926. Over the course of her visit to Ontario to attend the opening Carr met, exchanged views with, and was applauded by the Group of Seven. Lawren Harris's work made an immediate and profound impact on her. Reflecting on meeting the Group of Seven Carr wrote:

> I worked for history and cold fact. Next time I paint Indians I'm

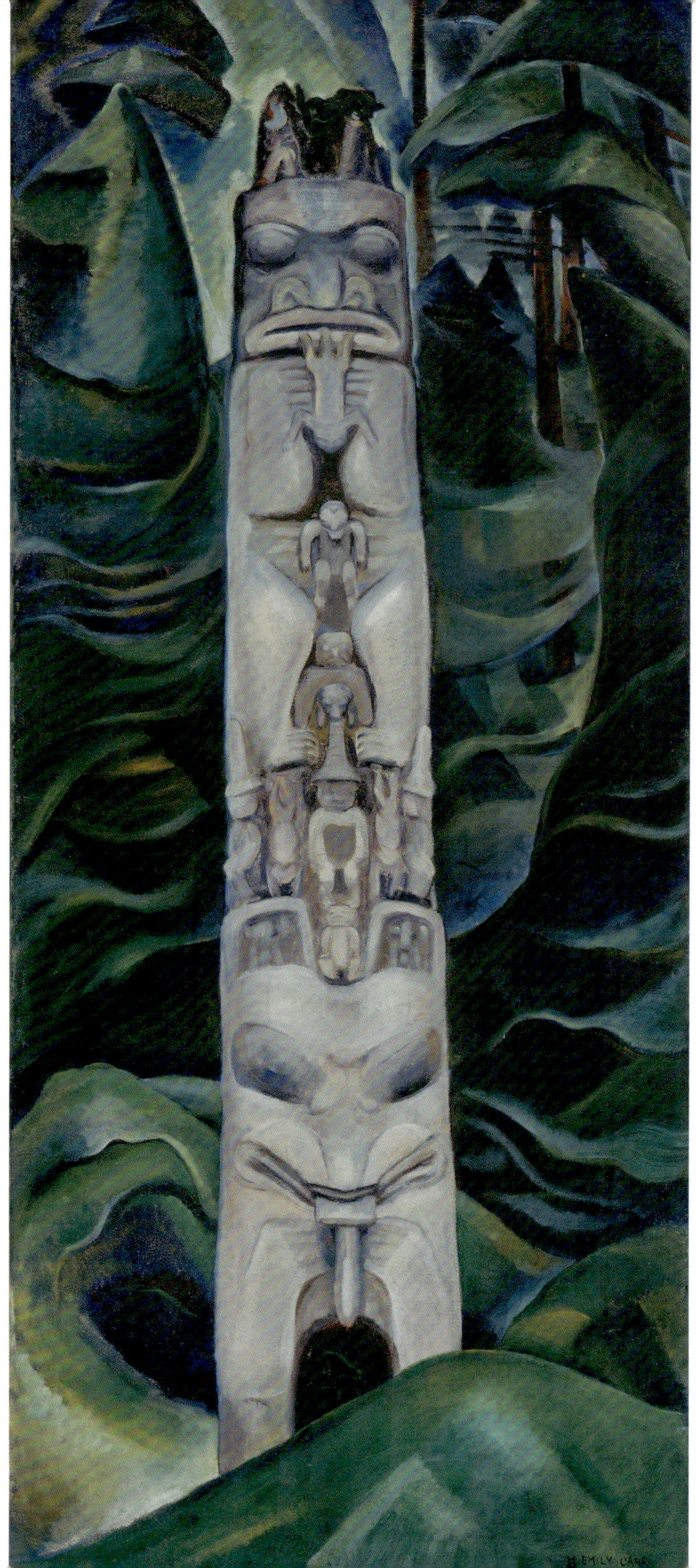
EMILY CARR

going off on a tangent tear. There is something bigger than fact: the underlying spirit...[15]

The enthusiasm Harris and other members of the Group of Seven had for her work was a tremendous boost for Carr. Inspired by the positive attention, the sales of her paintings, rugs, and pottery to and through the National Gallery, and the friendship offered by Lawren Harris, Marius Barbeau, and many others in Toronto and Ottawa, Carr returned to Victoria energized. Encouraging letters flew back and forth between Carr and Harris. With renewed vigour, Carr took up her First Nations quest with increased confidence and determination. In 1928, at the age of 56, she embarked on the most prolific period of her career, beginning with another ambitious six-week sketching trip to the Skeena River areas and Haida Gwaii, as well as to the Nass River and Gitanyow First Nations.

This trip was often difficult and even dangerous. Off the coast of Haida Gwaii, Carr was caught at sea in a storm that prevented her from sketching at Cumshewa and Tanu. Despite dreadful weather and problematic transportation, she revisited Skidegate and Skedans on Haida Gwaii and the Gitxsan communities on the Skeena. For the first time she was able to sketch the poles of the abandoned villages of Gitex and Angidar on the Nass, and spend valuable sketching time in Gitanyow (formerly Kitwancool.) Here, Carr created the watercolour *Mrs. Douse, Chieftainess of Kitwancool, c.1928*, the portrait of the hereditary chief. Carr presented a second portrait to her as a thank you for allowing her to stay and paint in the village.

Carr's 1928 trip was enormously gratifying and productive, resulting in masterful First Nations-themed paintings. Works from 1928–1931, such as *Totem and Forest*, 1931, indicate Carr consulted her sketches from 1912 and from 1928, and that she had learned much along the way from William and Clara Russ, Newcombe, Harris, and her own extensive reading. Carr's passion for both the Northwest Coast landscape and First Nations culture is clear. This painting of the frontal pole, which she had first seen and sketched in Haida Gwaii and then revisited in Prince Rupert in 1928 after its relocation, is a legible record of Haida artist Charles Edenshaw's family pole in which the Birth of the Bear clan is clearly articulated. Carr juxtaposes the pole with its natural environment—the forest—and invites us to consider the opening of the pole as the door into the forest, uniting First Nations subject matter and the environment in which it exists. Carr's paintings of 1928 show a strengthening of her main purpose: capturing the essence of her subject with smooth, sweeping brushwork, she emphasizes the important and eliminates the extraneous details. Employing an expressionist style, she concentrates on volume and form. Stylistic changes, especially the handling of light, reflect the influence of Lawren Harris and Seattle-based artist Mark Tobey.

The Modernist painter Mark Tobey visited Carr's guest house in 1928 and had a keen interest in, and his own personal collection of, American Indian art. Tobey had just returned from studying Cubism in France. Carr arranged for Tobey to give a workshop in her studio and temporarily became his student. *Big Eagle (Great Eagle), Skidigate, B.C., 1929*, is a fine example of Carr combining her 1912 and 1928 sketches of the Eagle pole in Qay'llnagaay with the Cubist approach of breaking up the picture plane into geometric forms.

Harris and Tobey suggested that Carr turn her attention from First Nations themes, but she was already heading in the direction of broadening her expression of First Nations subject matter. Carr was widening her vision of the spirit of Northwest Coast art: expressing the landscape and environment from which it arises. In 1929, Carr completed a sketching trip up the west coast of Vancouver Island to the Nuu-Chah-Nulth communities of Port Renfrew and Friendly Cove. One of the resulting canvases is Carr's *Indian Church*, 1929, purchased by Lawren Harris who was wildly enthusiastic about this expression of spirituality. Located at the historically significant site of first contact between Captain James Cook and the Nuu-Chah-Nulth people, this work attests to Carr's deep interest in the juxtaposition of First Nations spirituality with reference to both the environment and

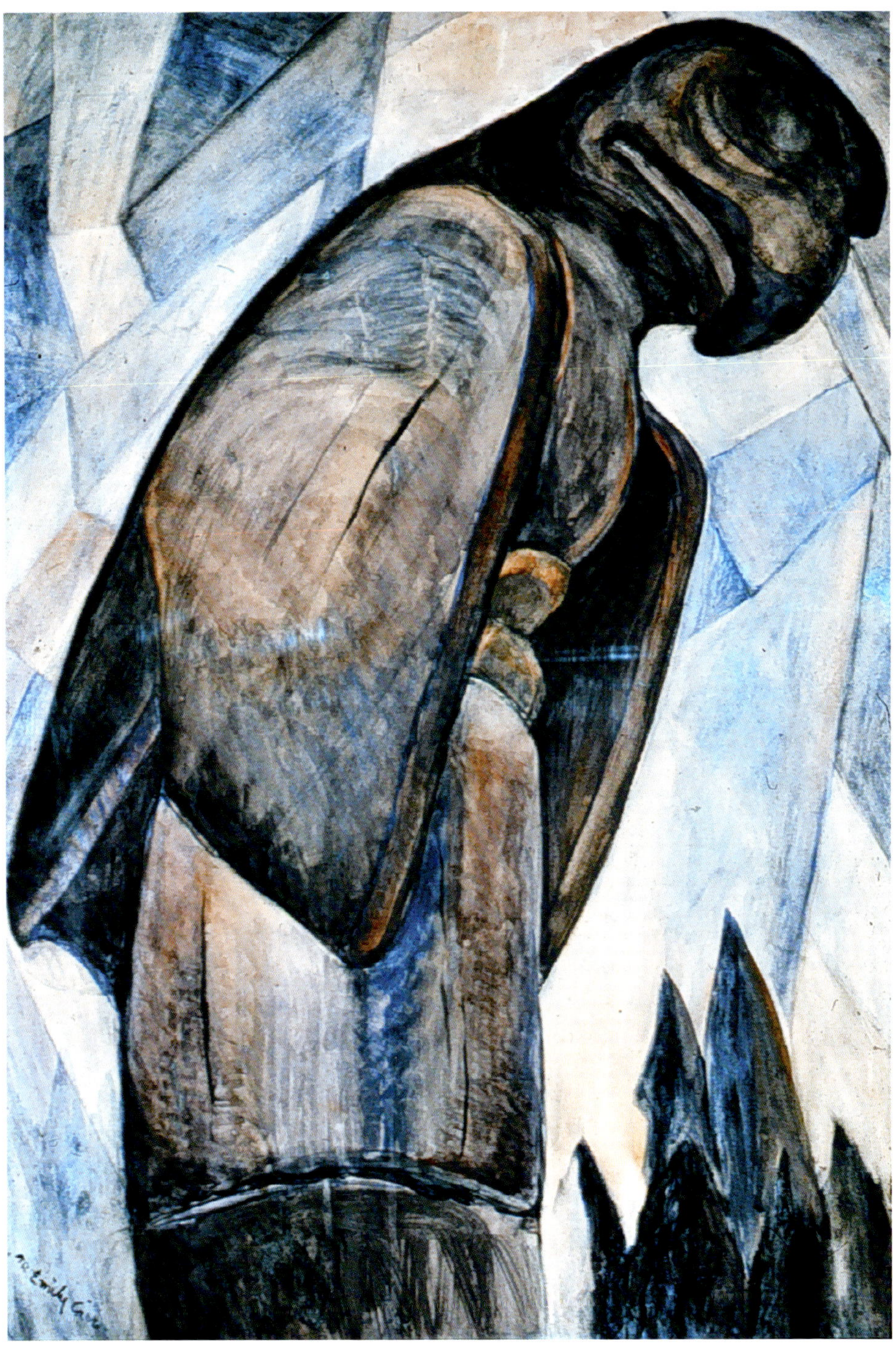

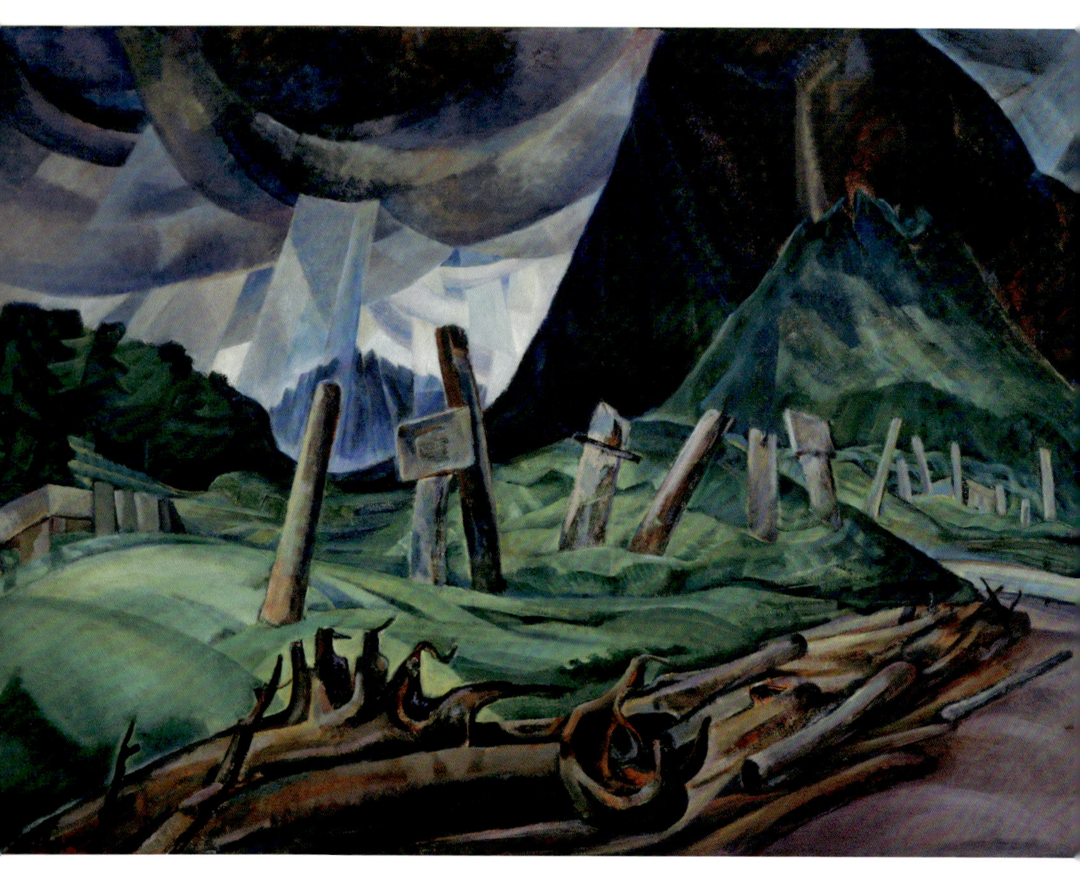

Vanquished, 1930, oil on canvas, 92.0 x 129.0 cm, Collection of the Vancouver Art Gallery, Emily Carr Trust VAG 42.3.6

PREVIOUS PAGE:
Big Eagle, (Great Eagle), Skidigate, B.C., 1929, watercolour on paper 76.2 x 56.7 cm, The Art Gallery of Greater Victoria, Donated in memory of Dorothy Plaunt Dyde 1980.034.001

the imported Christianity of the newcomers. Carr was experimenting with theosophical concepts with reference to her links with First Nations people and the environment of British Columbia, especially the precept of direct apprehension of the Divine through nature.

Other major works between 1929 and 1931 include *Vanquished, 1930*, a strong statement of the abandoned village of Skedans on Haida Gwaii. This painting represents another example of Carr integrating her passion for First Nations cultures and the British Columbian landscape. It is a political statement about the realities then facing the Haida people. The Haida mortuary poles are being reclaimed by Nature; the village is in mourning. Smallpox had virtually wiped out this village. It is an homage and also, through the symbolism of the powerful landscape and beams of light, a message of hope for renewal.

The 1930s were prolific years for Carr who found her development of oils on paper, a liberating and inexpensive medium. The Depression curtailed her sketching activities, but she did travel to the Kwakwaka'wakw villages of Koskimo and Fort Rupert on northern Vancouver Island in 1930, and to the interior Coast Salish communities of Brackendale and Lillooett in 1933, which resulted in major oil on canvas works. Sketching trips after 1933 were close to home. Having purchased a caravan in 1933 that she named the Elephant, Carr could live in "the heart" of what she loved. Goldstream Park, an important Coast Salish salmon fishing site, was a favourite spot. Carr sketched in the day and wrote stories at night that included reminiscences of her many travels up the Coast.

The series of Forest Interior and Sea and Sky paintings from these years are expressions of her passionate attachment to nature and the spiritual awakening stimulated by the British Columbia environment. Carr was overcome by the energy and all-encompassing rejuvenation of nature. While rejecting theosophy in favour of her own brand of Christianity, she still found God in nature. The joy and exaltation expressed in her paintings come from this personal connection to both First Nations cultures and the environment.

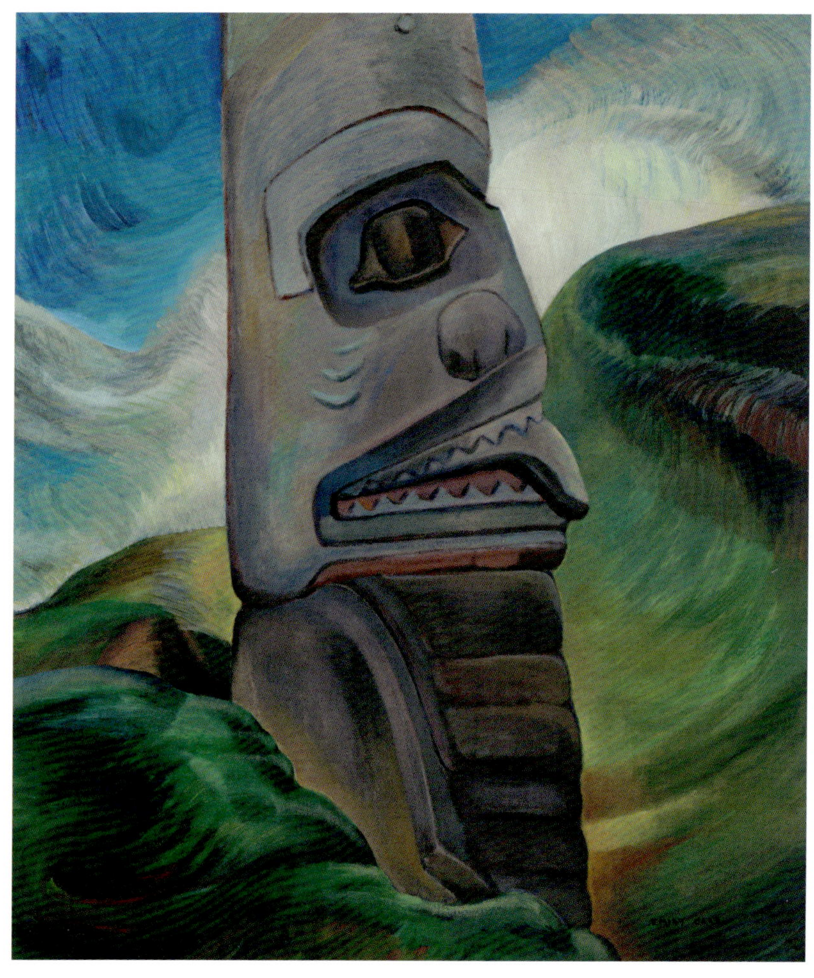

A Skidegate Pole, 1942, oil on canvas, 87.0 x 76.5 cm, Collection of the Vancouver Art Gallery, Emily Carr Trust VAG 42.3.37

In 1936, Carr unburdened herself of the "House of All Sorts," but the relief was short lived. The upheaval of the move, coupled with increasing poor health, culminated in a massive heart attack in January of 1937. Significantly, one of the few completed paintings of this year is *Forsaken*, 1937, an oil painting of a Wolf Clan mortuary pole from Angidar on the Nass River that she had visited and sketched in 1928. The pole had since been removed to Ottawa. Once again, Carr provides us with a record of a pole, this time of the Nisga'a, in its original context and a statement about the realities of disruption among First Nations peoples.

Carr's series of heart attacks and strokes between 1937 and 1944 confined her to bed much of the time, but in her journals she tells us that her mind and spirit travelled to much loved First Nations villages. At times too weak to stand and paint, Carr devoted most of her creative energies to writing. Regaining strength, she created a whole new body of First Nations paintings, such as *Kitwancool Poles*, c. 1940 in part born of her writings. Her book *Klee Wyck* was released in 1941 in time for Carr's 70th birthday. The widely acclaimed best-seller received the Governor General's award for non-fiction in 1942, which not only thrilled Carr but kept her First Nations subject matter in the forefront. Many of her final oil on paper sketches of 1944, just months before her death, reveal a subtle integration of First Nations and landscape concerns. Woven into the carved-like foliage the mischievous *Shup-Shup* of Coast Salish culture is peeking out. Two of Carr's last oil-on-canvas paintings are *Clearing*, 1942, a landscape based on her last sketching trip to Mount Douglas, a spiritually significant mountain for Coast Salish people, and *A Skidegate Pole*, 1942 where she had sketched enthusiastically in 1912 and 1928. *A Skidegate Pole* is a final statement—strong, assured, and complete. The Haida pole segment, nestled in its coastal spot and emphasizing the Dogfish crest, stands as a testament to Carr's enduring affinity and intense interest in First Nations cultures.

ENDNOTES

1 Lawren Harris to Emily Carr, March, 1930, correspondence in private collection, Victoria, BC.

2 Jean Barman, *The West Beyond the West*, (Toronto: University of Toronto Press) 1994, p. 263.

3 BC Archives, MS-2181, Emily Carr, Box 2, Folio 16, Journal 3, February 22, 1930.

4 BC Archives, MS-0610, Richard Carr, Diary 1836–1881.

5 Sir James Douglas, The Hudson's Bay Company's Chief Factor at Fort Victoria declared in 1843 that the site of Beacon Hill Park was a "perfect Eden." See Richard Mackie, *Trading Beyond the Mountains: the British Fur Trade on the Pacific 1793-1843*, (Vancouver: University of British Columbia Press) 1997, p. 279. For Camus cultivation see: Nancy Turner, *Plant Technology of First Peoples in British Columbia*, Vancouver: University of British Columbia Press, 2001.

6 Emily Carr, *Growing Pains: The Autobiography of Emily Carr*, (Toronto: Clarke, Irwin) 1966, p. 211.

7 Aldona Jonaitis, *Art of the Northwest Coast*, (Seattle: University of Washington Press) 2006, p. 182.

8 Emily Carr, *Growing Pains*, p. 211.

9 BC Archives, MS-2181, Emily Carr, Box 7, Folio 33/4, Notebook on Totems, 1913.

10 Douglas Cole, *Captured Heritage: the Scramble for Northwest Coast Artifacts*, Vancouver, UBC. Press, 1985, 272-277. See also Ron Hawker's, *Tales of Ghosts: First Nations Art in British Columbia, 1922-61*, (Vancouver: UBC Press) 2003.

11 Jamie Morton. "Tanu and Skedans Ethnohistory Project: Background Notes from Documentary Sources," Manuscript Report prepared for Canadian Parks and Queen Charlotte Islands Museum, 1993.

12 Michael Breuer and Kerry Mason (Dodd), *Sunlight in the Shadows*, (Toronto: Oxford University Press) 1984, p. 7.

13 Maria Tippett, *Emily Carr: A Bbiography*, (Toronto: Stoddart Publishing) 1994, p. 136.

14 Charles C. Hill, *Emily Carr: New Perspectives*, (Ottawa/Vancouver: National Gallery and Vancouver Art Gallery) 2006, pp 94-155

15 BC Archives, MS-2181, Emily Carr, Box 2, Folio 14, Journal 1, November 14, 1927.

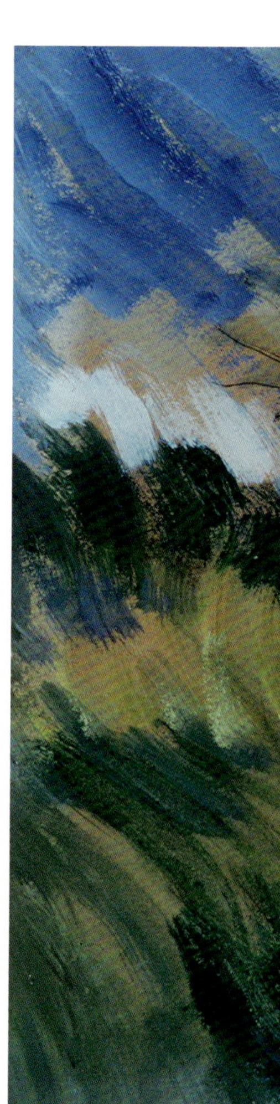

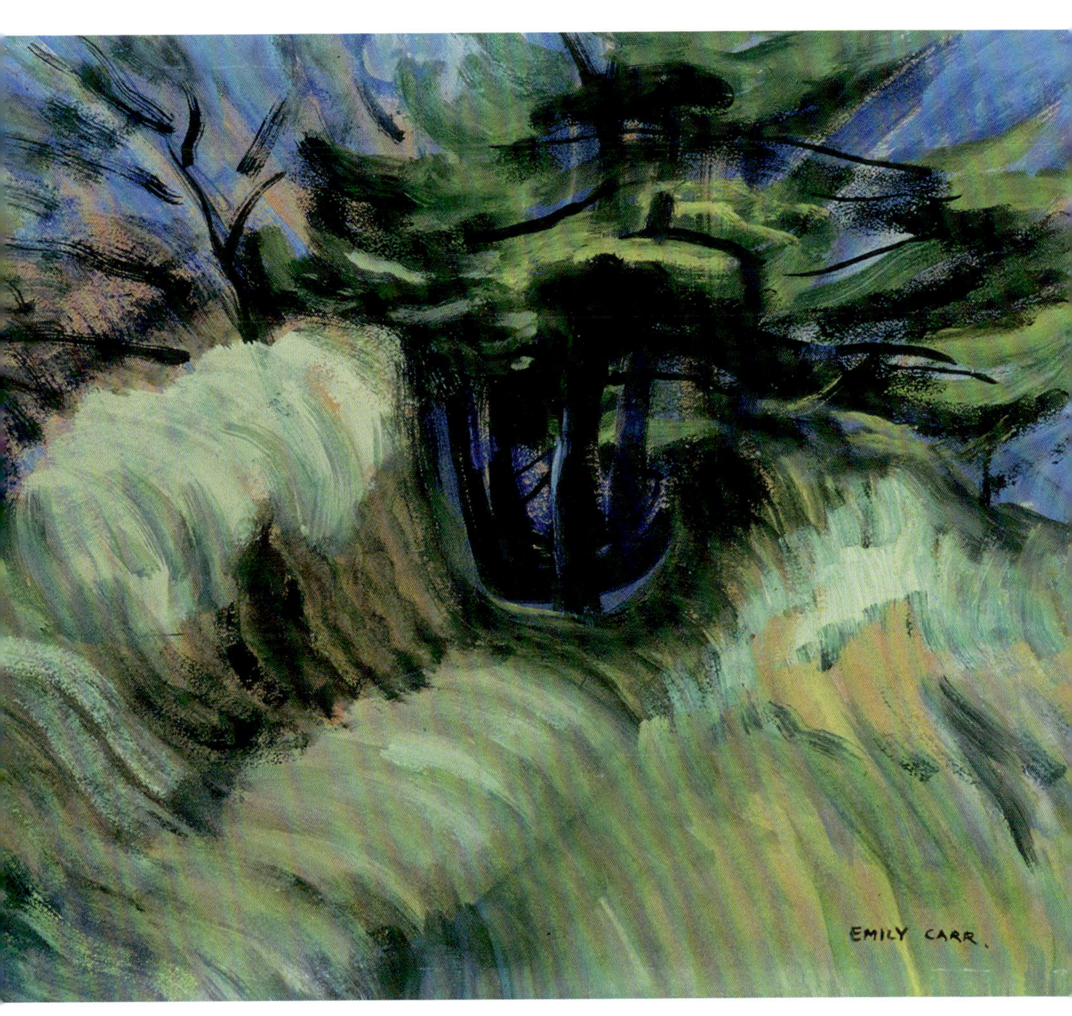

Broom, Beacon Hill, 1937, oil on paper mounted on board, 29.5 x 43.1 cm
The Art Gallery of Greater Victoria, The Thomas Gardiner Keir Bequest 1994.055.006

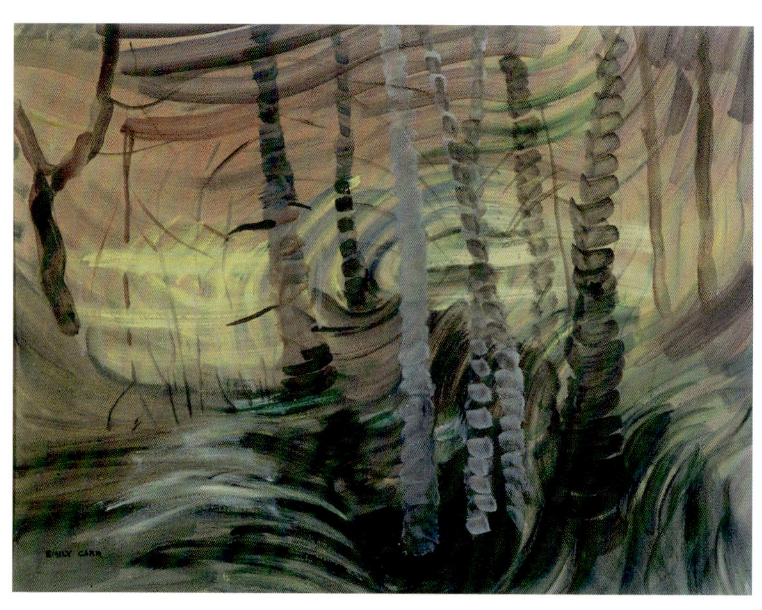
EMILY CARR

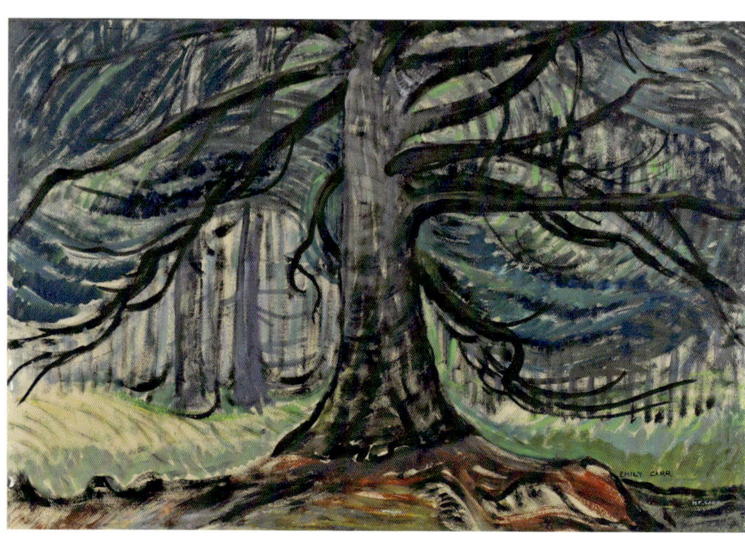
EMILY CARR

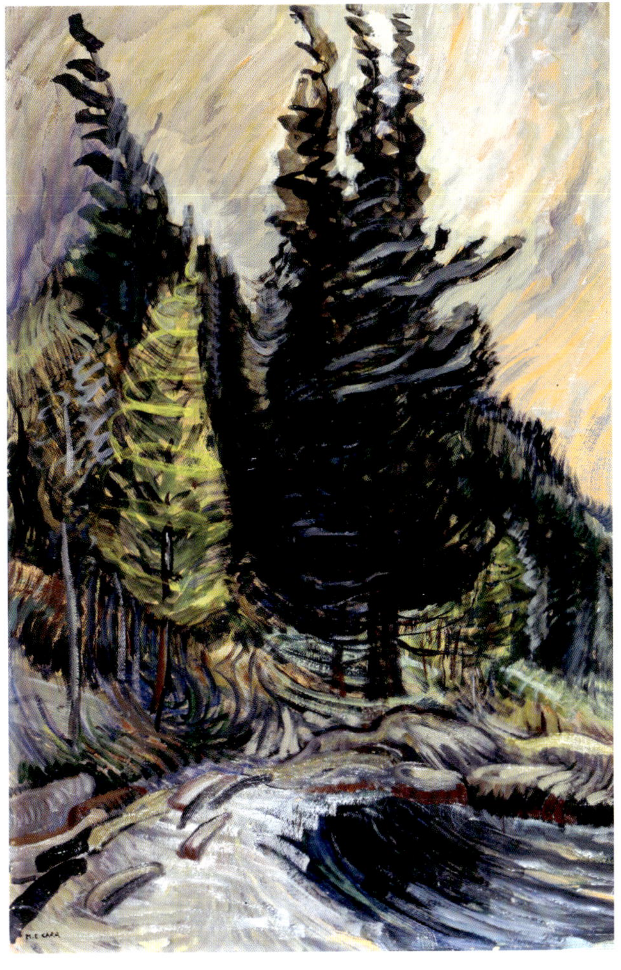

Spring, c.1936-1937, oil on paper, 45.2 x 60.2 cm, The Art Gallery of Greater Victoria, Ruth Humphrey Estate 1984.050.001

Dancing Tree, c.1938, oil on paper, 61.1 x 91.6 cm, The Art Gallery of Greater Victoria, Gift of the Hon. Mark Kearly in memory of Mabel Florence Kearley 1968.212.001

Trees, c.1932, oil on paper mounted on board, 88.8 x 58.4 cm, The Art Gallery of Greater Victoria, Gift of Donald and Nadine Lawson 2000.011.001

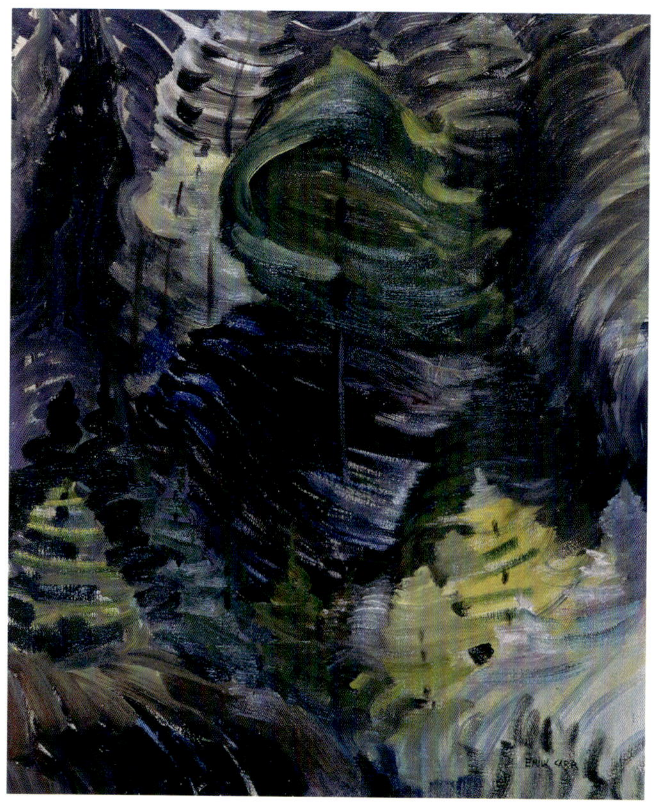

Juice of Life, 1938-1939, oil on canvas, 64.4 x 52.7 cm, The Art Gallery of Greater Victoria, Bequest of Dr. Ethlyn Trapp, Vancouver 1973.225.001

Wooded Hillside, c.1929-1930, charcoal on paper, 44.2 x 31.5 cm, The Art Gallery of Greater Victoria, Gift of George and Lola Kidd 1998.028.001

Untitled (Sketch of Trees), c.1930, graphite on paper, 15.0 x 22.8 cm The Art Gallery of Greater Victoria, Gift of Mr. Peter Ohler 1973.069.001

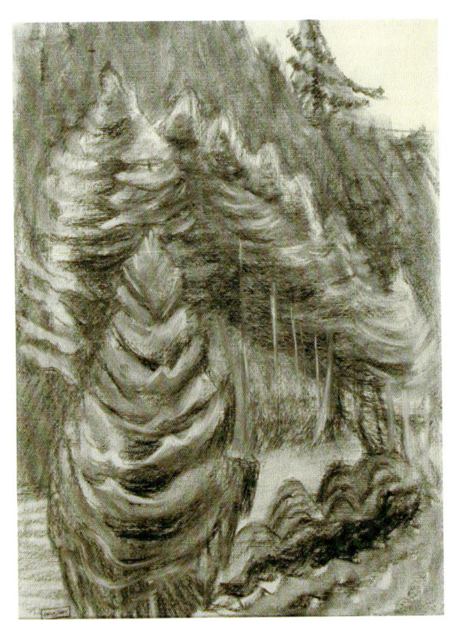

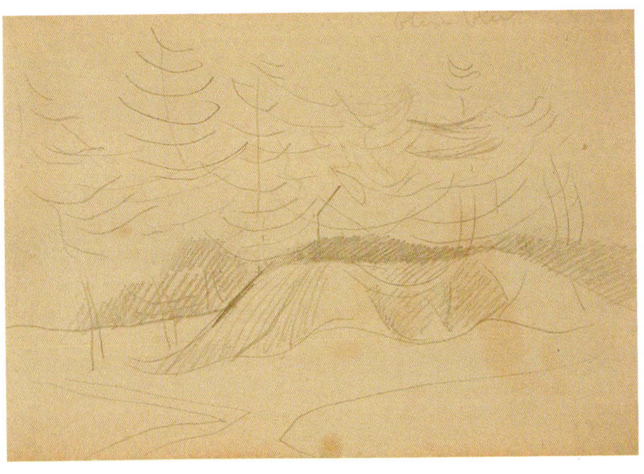

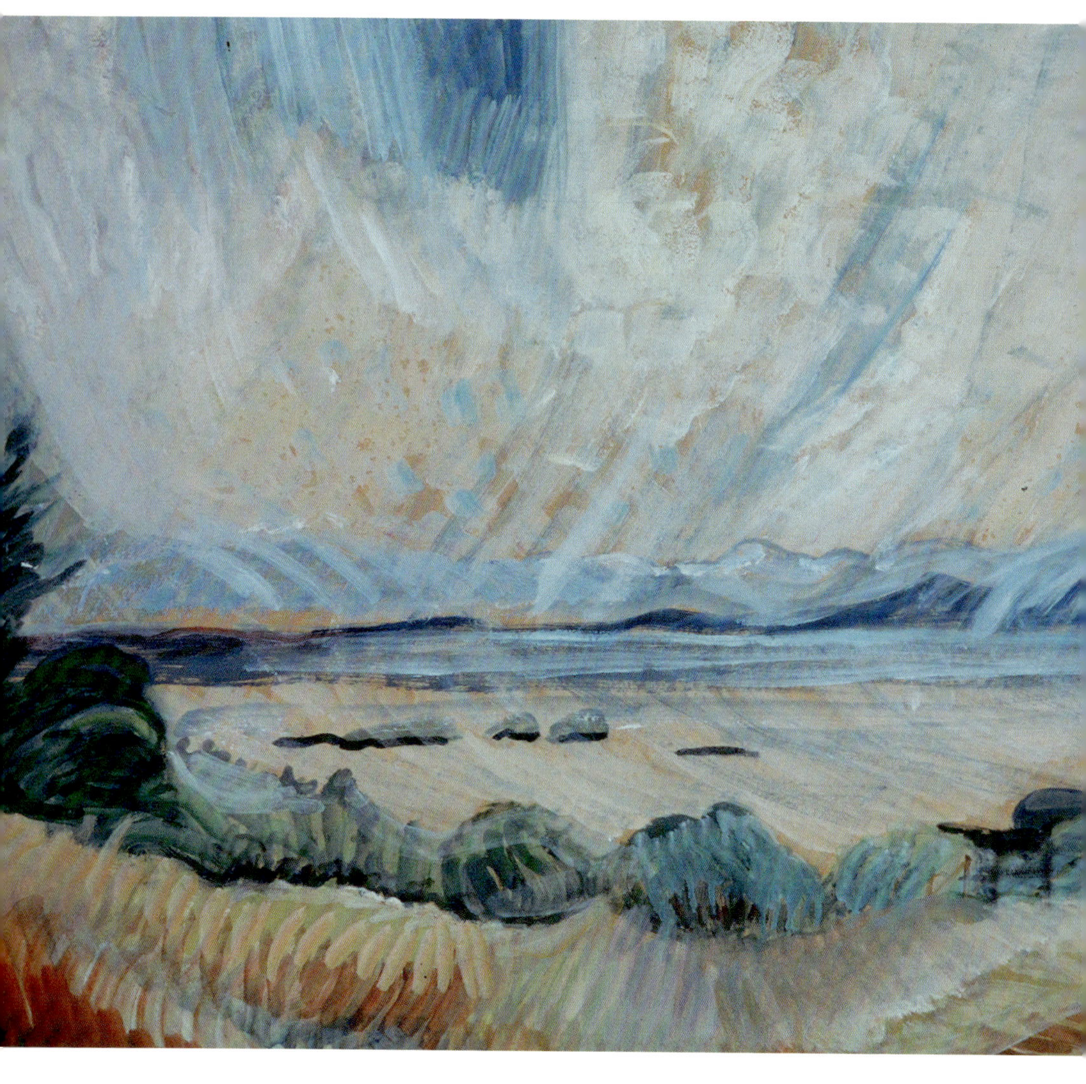

Lagoon at Albert Head, c.1940, oil on paper, 51.5 x 72.5 cm, The Art Gallery of Greater Victoria, The Thomas Gardiner Keir Bequest 1994.055.003

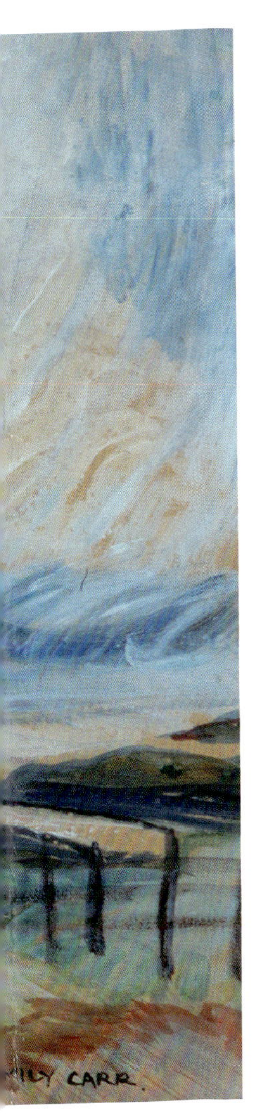

Suggested Reading

Blanchard, Paula, *The Life of Emily Carr*. Vancouver: Douglas & McIntyre, 1987.

Carr, Emily, *Hundreds and Thousands: The Journals of Emily Carr*. Toronto: Clark, Irwin, 1966.

Carr, Emily, *Klee Wyck*. Toronto: Oxford University Press, 1941.

*Emily Carr wrote several other books worth reading including *Book of Small*, *Growing Pains*, and *The House of All Sorts*.

Dodd, Kerry Mason, *Sunlight in the Shadows: The Landscape of Emily Carr*. Toronto: Oxford University Press, 1984.

Hill, Charles, Johanne Lamoureux, Ian Thom, et al., *Emily Carr: New Perspectives on a Canadian Icon*. Ottawa: National Gallery of Canada and Vancouver Art Gallery, 2006.

Shadbolt, Doris, *Emily Carr*. Vancouver: Douglas & McIntyre Ltd., 1990.

Tippett, Maria, Emily *Carr: A Biography*. Toronto: Oxford University Press, 1979.

Vancouver Art Gallery Emily Carr Website: http://www.virtualmuseum.ca/Exhibitions/EmilyCarr/

Credits

Exhibition Curator: Mary Jo Hughes
Contributing writer and consultant: Kerry Mason
Publication Project Manager: Mary Jo Hughes
Editor: Joan Padgett
Publication Designer: Frank Reimer
Photographer: Stephen Topfer (unless otherwise indicated)
Printer: Friesens Corp.

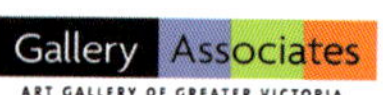

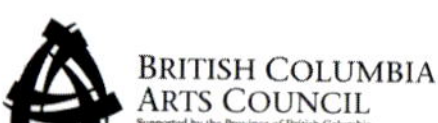

Canada Council for the Arts
Conseil des Arts du Canada

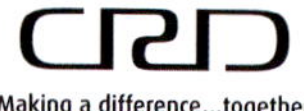
Making a difference...together

Art Gallery of Greater Victoria
1040 Moss Street
Victoria, British Columbia
Canada V8V 4P1
1-250-384-4171 aggv.ca